Spirit 5
The Beginning
INTRODUCTION

I have created four super human characters the first is Benjamin and he is the spirit five, an assassin from the world that looks over the planet earth. How I created him, I guess it was through the thought though my mind the idea was that he was to eliminate seven extremely important people who had miss used their judgement and powers governing the planet earth they were to be punished. As every superhero has a story there is a good part and a bad part one minute he would be doing things for the good and other times he would be doing thing for the bad. The hero in this story is all bad in his case the bad guys win and there is a curse to go with it as Benjamin must live with the five super powers that process him. In this case it is the same, but there is a story to it.
I do not know how I came about it, one minute I was sitting there on my stool writing in the dark the next minute I had created him Benjamin. Benjamin is the spirit. On top of this I had some more characters that I had created. I decided at the time that the story needed a bit of help, so I decided to add a couple of futuristic coppers called the oxygen and the hitman and gave them a car called the cool one, after the number plate which was private on their car, Benjamin is close to it as it is close to the public. They do not like it, there must be bad guys in the story and there both it. not forgetting the real master, the silhouette, a sassy cool individual and killer that brings Benjamin down a good looking cool adversary that has the power to bring the Benjamin down he that bad guy in the story. Who will win, who knows yet have a read.
As I continue, Benjamin knows that there is something going on in planet earth and that's the only reason that he is there. Benjamin has some help from his friends a robot that we call a robot some of the time and other time's we call him mar arty and a couple of crazy sun flowers called the flowers to guide him.

Preface

Benjamin knows that there is something wrong on the planet earth the story go's he is busy moving to a new house he is upstairs in his attic. As he clears the boxes in his attic he stumbles getting ready to move he stubbles across an old tin at first, he ignores it but the feeling that the tin gave him drew him back to it, so he puts it aside for another time except he is drawn to it more the more he tries to disregard the thought the more his mind thinks about it. he is extremely drawn to it. as the next few days past looking at the box he decides to open it and when he doe's he finds a magic badge. This badge is extremely special and once it is on you it cannot be removed from the clothing and will slowly become part of the body. Benjamin does not know this at first, Benjamin decides to fly to Britain to a professor to find the meaning of the badge and wants to know what exactly what it's purpose.

Spirit five
THE BEGINING
Chapter one

It was the lion that praises before it makes a kill, I had to make seven hits on planet earth. The first was a business man the second was a holy man and the third was a position. I came from OutSpace another planet and I was obeying my orders. I was blessed with five super human powers hence the badge that I was wearing, I was told to use the badge as a weapon and away of escape if I got in to trouble. I was not the good guy in this war, I was a killer, I was the assassin, the ultimate weapon. As I sat down in my arm chair in my space craft thirty thousand feet below the Atlantic Ocean, I was deep in thought over the thought of how I was going to make the first move in fact in the end it was going to be the other way around. I had forgotten to put the ship in stealth I was pick up on the radar of a us vasal a submarine two in fact. These people do not mess around and I was thinking I should blow them out of the water. I got the message

CAPTAIN: "we have an undefinable object on our radars precede code red."

OFFICER: "Ready when you are sir."

CAPTAIN: "Send a message of peace to them whoever they are remind them that they are in our waters."

OFFICER: "Okay captain."

Benjamin calls for his robot from out the back of his ship, he is busy watering the flowers

BENJAMIN: "Yes I did, keep the u boat company while I decide what to do."

Before Benjamin has a chance to think the robot butts in.

THE ROBOT: "According to my calculations we have three options the first is to attack them the second we can surface which will only cause a stand by and the third we can stay put there is a sixty percent chance of getting away if our stealth is working, they will not pick us up on their radar and we could float right by."

BENJAMIN: "That is a lot of words for a robot. Give me some therapy."
THE ROBOT: "Well of course we are both nuts."
The robot continues: "Energy levels are low we are not going to make it as the oxygen levels are to low also I am sorry to say Benjamin that we have no choice but to surface."
BENJAMIN: "I hope your right okay send her up."
THE ROBOT: "Hay man I do not make mistakes."
BENJAMIN: "Take her up to the top."

In the back ground the two sun flowers are discussing the incident.
SUNFLOWER ONE: "Were going on an adventure."
SUN FLOWER TWO: "no we are not we are surfacing."
SUNFLOWER ONE:" It is still an adventure."
Benjamin takes control of the vesicle taking his machine up two thousand meters fast knowing that the two trident submarines would be waiting for him at the top of the ocean and would follow him.
As Benjamin slowly rises and out of the water's surface his space ship sits in-between the two subs.

With both submarine s by his sides he is hailed by them both captain s, the first stands on board and tries to make contact Benjamin refuses to answer, as he is hailed again he can feel the pressure as he is watching more and more soldiers appear on the subs decks either side of Benjamin and armed the commandos are called to their bridge signalling each other. Benjamin spacecraft is just hovering above the sea level, with no cause of action the submarine on the right side of him opens fire sending the submarine on the left side of Benjamin and his space ship in to chaos. There soldiers shouting and bumping each other off their submarines and into the oceans, there was an array of missiles which were sent to the spacecraft soon afterwards, Benjamin speaks to his systems.

BENJAMIN: "Vertical systems position computer. Hold tight".

The computer confers its orders and quickly becomes vertically up right within a few seconds it launches itself up into the hemisphere, a cool escape. Benjamin thinks so.

THE COMMANDER: "Well I have never seen anything like that before."

The submarines return to the underneath of the ocean.

CHAPTER TWO
TWENTY-FOUR HOURS AWAY

Benjamin is back in space about twenty-four hours away from his target. Zero gravity, as he floats around his space ship fixing things, it's damage and thinking how he was going to do the dirty work ahead of him. As he floats towards his computer and sitting down turning the system on the flicks through the video footage, images and looking hard at them and planning how he was going to meet the first target, how he would approach him on the earth to make the kill.

Benjamin did not know that the British fleet that he meet had been filming him and within a few days of the incident it was all over the news and all over the world. There was headline s such as alien vasal surfaces and other quotes the earth has been invaded and unidentified spaceship harbours sea and other stuff like naval officer's sink after seeing mysterious ship found at sea and so on. Benjamin knew that it was now a silly time to approach the planet again at this time and if it was not for the ships damage he would have made the hit sooner. He had only had a few hours to make it back to the earth. Benjamin was thinking that he was going to miss the hit all together the targets time to die was only a few hours away.

It had to be timed perfection, Benjamin knew this he had too there was a time on everything that he did on that day it had a purpose a meaning and he knew that he would only get one chance, he could not afford to miss it. as the hours turned into minutes he was going to attempt the approach to planet earth.

BENJAMIN: "Give me a visual on planet earth please."

He speaks to his computer

BENJAMIN: "Visual. Visual recovered scan area for required address and home destination.

We are on our way."

Benjamin slowly takes control of the space ship pushing a few buttons here and there and a few switches taking control of the spaceship. Taking it to the earth and planet.

BENJAMIN: "What's the time please."

THE ROBOT: "It is exactly five minutes to twelve o'clock in the evening."
Benjamin only had five minutes to find him the clock was ticking fast Benjamin tells his computer to go to hyper speed stealth they were at the target in a jiffy.

A few second s later Benjamin sees his target and the game was on. Benjamin was waiting for the weather change it was by god that the weather would work on my behalf. As I approached the planet earth I got lower it was a rough landing as the weather as I said changed rapidly too hot to cold with a long dark sky to go with it. it was getting cloudier and it had begun to rain. By the time that I had settled the ship down I was ready for the target. The target that I had not mentioned until now was of significant important it was the mayor of the city of angles, LA. I have been there before and have fond memories as I landed the ship, the ship had a heat sensor scanning device infer red to scan the building for the target within a few minutes I had found him. I was watching him, but I had company which I knew as my robot had my back.
THE ROBOT: "Five you have company. There's a verse in the ally way beside of you with the words COOL ONE on the number plate do you recognise it."
BENJAMIN: "No I do not."
THE ROBOT:" I| have tried the profile but I am getting nothing."
Benjamin replies that is now aware and is moving in on the target and he is content on hunting down the mayor.
The robot's instinct is being to tell Benjamin not to make the move, but Benjamin refuses to listen he says it is too close and wants his target.

It did not take too long for the cool one to find Benjamin systems and they were both on to him that's the hitman and the oxygen. Benjamin ship was now on the ground with not a lot of room to manuver.
Benjamin watches intensively the two cops sitting in their cool one but not as cool as a space ship benjamin says to himself. Oxygen undoes the window as he smokes a cigarette.
HITMAN: "Do you know that really stinks."
OXYGEN: "I heard it was really bad for you. Your breath too. "
HITMAN: "Yeah well do not tell the wife. You must have a really sweet kiss."
OXYGEN: "Is this our guy."
HITMAN: "Probably he looks like the disruption, he looks like he has just cloaked his ship."
OXYGEN:" I think that we should give him a welcome."
Benjamin heard the whole conversation, he continues to his computer.
BENJAMIN: "Computer arm rockets on target and full shields."
The cool one's car was also armoured also Benjamin takes a chance and at the last second that the target had changed. Benjamin is in two minds he knows that the real target is the mayor, but the two cool coppers were on their way also just for being in the wrong place at the wrong time.
Benjamin knows that he has been seen and must make a split decision, he must decide if he should make the first move he is communicating with his robot who is on his space ship for a quick report on the situation the robots reply ids that he has a fifty/ fifty chance of reaching his targets now that there are three of them. It was clear to Benjamin that the cool one and its passengers were in Benjamin's way. Benjamin could not kill in cold blood there had to be a reason but however if the cool one made the first move. By the laws of

Benjamin's planet, he could put it through his council, and defend himself. It would be by luck if the two cops made the first move in fact they were probably thinking the same as him. There was a long silence within Benjamin as he study's them form a distance knowing that they could not see him.

Benjamin speaks to his robot.

BENJAMIN: "Am I clear."

THE ROBOT:" No you have company and it looks like you have a lot it. There is car parked about two hundred feet from you over the voice indicator it sound s like the cops and above you a helicopter and it looks like some cops on the street are approaching you."

Benjamin says to himself that he can do it even though he thinks that the target has too much cover then changes his mind. And says to himself that he thinks that he should go. Benjamin loses the first round. Not thinking he believes that he has lost until he receives a message about the badge he had totally forgot even so now it was too late he was uncertain, and he just wanted to get out of and off the streets, but his consciousness kept on telling him to use the badge.

BENJAMIN:" How stupid is this this is useless it's not going to work."

CONSIOUSNESS: "Use the badge. You have to believe."

BENJAMIN: "This is rubbish I prefer the old-fashioned way, you know guns at dawn and all the other stuff. So, what do you want me to do step inside the future."

CONSIOUSNESS. "It is your future."

Benjamin stops for a second as he is now back on the space craft as he walks on he walks back off almost straight away.

BENJAMIN: "I'm going outside and I'm going to nail this guy. Open the doors."

Benjamin welding his space gun leaves the ship walking like an assassin would walk he heads towards the building, he already knows who the target is all he needs to know is where his target is in the building. Benjamin has not already got use to his badge or the gun as they are gifts, but he knew deep down inside that he would use his new powers wisely and it would take time to perfect them and he would have to sue them in the end if he wanted to survive in the end.

Benjamin walks into the office building as he pushes the door open the cool one down the street tells the oxygen that the building has company as an armed man has entered the building. Benjamin already knows that he has been seen and takes the chance that he could make the hit there are people everywhere Benjamin speaks to his robot telling him that he is well protected as he continues to look for the target. The robot tells Benjamin to press his badge a couple of times Benjamin tells him that he is sound with his gun, but the robot overrides his mission and tells him to hurry up and press the badge, finally Benjamin listens as he presses the spirit five badge twice he changes in to a tiger he changes quickly in to the forces beast. The people in the building were just standing watching him as he moved through the people some pointing other running to get out of his way as this is happening fast the cool one and the two cops turn up you would think in the nick of time, but they were too late also.

OXYGEN: "Guns out, time to party."

Oxygen draws first trying to get a scope on the tiger who was Benjamin, Oxygen is also speaking to the hitman who in touch with the cool one just outside the building. Benjamin knows that the two cops mean business too, he morphs back to his human form as the people innocent people all leave the building as they were allowed Benjamin makes his way up stairs to the mayor's office the two cops are following him. The mayor was an easy target. When Benjamin walked into the office the mayor was sitting at his desk. He spoke quietly.

THE MAYOR:" I knew that you were coming."

As the mayor took another line of the substance that he was putting up his nose he continues.

THE MAYOR: "What did I do."

I could tell he was sorry, but I was not there to play god, I was not the person to do the forgiving all I could say was to him was that it was not man who has the power to forgive that was god. I looked at him once more as he took another line through a note it looked to me if he was trying to OD before I filled him with bullets. I could hear the engine of the cool one just outside I knew that I would have some company on the way out. And I also knew that the two cops were heading my way. I suppose I could call it gods victim.

BENJAMIN:" Hard luck your dead."

Benjamin pulls his gun out of his holster and with cause of concern puts a couple of bullets in him two to the chest he was dead. Benjamin did not need to leave a calling card. He thinks that the police would get the message. The power of Benjamin's gun went right through him and the window four feet behind him the sound echoed through the walls of the building, giving the two cops Benjamin's where about. Benjamin was clever enough to figure out the rest he leaps over the body of the dead guy, the mayor and out of the shattered window as the cops enter the room landing on top of the three-parked private numbered police car. He makes a smooth landing as he uncloaks his space ship and makes it back on foot. Benjamin speaks to himself saying the old-fashioned phase one down six to go. He continues talking to himself trying to explain to himself what he had done he was feeling high it was bit of a buzz. He continued that the fall from the window was incredible, he had made it back to his space ship and was still talking about the experience

BENJAMIN: "That was a hundred-foot drop. I do not know how I did it, but I did it, has to be this space costume."

The robot butts in.

ROBOT: "It is not a costume it is a suit, wear it with pride, you're the spirit five."

The robot continues: "It is made of in destructible material through the badge."

Mean time while Benjamin is back on his space ship looking for some fresh air and taking a breather from his life the two coppers are weighing up the pro s and cons off the maximum carnage of what the spirit five had left behind.

OXYGEN: "We've missed him he's long gone with a smile on his face."

HITMAN: "I'm going to call it in maybe somebody out there might had seen something."

OXYGEN:" This guy in front of me is dead he is the mayor, why him?

HITMAN: "I do not know are the drugs on the table his or is this a set up

OXYGEN: "I'll run it through forensic, it looks to me like murder two bullets to the chest."

HITMAN: "Is there anything else."

OXYGEN: "Two shots unregistered gun two bullets to the chest."

HITMAN: "We should have waited how did he escape."

OXYGEN:" No, we should have waited, how did he escape."

HITMAN:" It looked like he jumped out of the window after he but a couple of bullets through it."
OXYGEN: I'll take some photographs you go down stairs and see if he's has left another mess."
HITMAN: "OKAY."
OXYGEN: "Oh and call the medics and tell them to come and collect this they have got a mess on their hands."

Benjamin before that conversation was boasting how somehow, he miraculously landed on his feet after the large leap on to his space craft. He rolled onto his feet, he orders marri arty the robot to open the cargo doors and steps upon the ship.
BENJAMIN: "Job done."
MARRIARTY: "Yes job done, let's get out of here."
Benjamin walks through the spaceship to his cockpit, he shows no remorse as for what just happened as it was by order of the council he buckles up sitting in his space chair and leaves the planet only to know that he would be back and does not know that the two cops and the cool one will be waiting for him or even more so that they had been watching. He was now a target the hunter becoming the hunted.

CHAPTER THREE
THE REVERSE

For the killing of the mayor la that's loss angles the city of angles Benjamin is offered by his councils some time off. As he is standing in front of the council and is questioned. The council needed all the information all the details of what had just taken place on the planet earth. As they insisted that everything they do is by god as the planet is by god but not the earth they have different rules.
The first councillor starts the discussion
FRIST COUNCILLOR ANTHONY: "how did you do it."?
BENJAMIN:" I used the suit."
SECOND COUNTCILLOR ANTHONY: "When did you make contact."?
They had to make that everything that I did was done was done by their law in a way that binds them to their law.
BENJAMIN: "Of I did he was snuffing something up his nose he was stuffing his face with narcotics it was obvious he knew that I was on my way to him."
COUNTCILLOR ANDREW: "What was said."?
BENJAMIN: Not a lot by the time I had got there up in the mayor's room the cops had picked up my signal through their car apparently called the cool one that's what I hear through the grape vine. It has good technology but not advanced as ours I was making my way upstairs."
As Benjamin spoke he was slowly beginning to feel out of place with the questioning' it was like he was on trial and not the victim on trial which he was unsettling. He had no choice but to continue.
BENJAMIN: "Everything that I did on that day was by your law. I played by your rules and know you bring me here. M y robot has video footage of my every move, you have nothing on me or my crew. My robot has recorded everything that has happened if you do not believe in me then turn to my computer the evidence will be the same as I have just spoke. I was doing my job."

MARRIERTY: "I have to agree."

Benjamin continues:" I found the target which was the mayor of New York, as requested and I ill mated him as requested I killed him like I was ordered. The worlds a better place."
COUNTCILLOR ANDREW: "Did you speak to the victim.""?
BENJAMIN: "No I played him two bullets to the chest as my computer ordered."
COUNTCILLOR ANTHONY:" What happened when you first entered the building.""?

Benjamin is beginning to feel uneasy about the questioning, but he continues to answer their questions.
BENJAMIN: "There was lots of people around mainly a lot of office workers, at that point I had to use my badge and I morphed into a tiger by touching my badge to scare them aside, I then morphed again changing myself back to my human form by thinking about it through my mind."
The badge being controlled by my robot also inside the space ship.
COUNTCILLOR ANDERW: "Well it seems that you have done everything within yours powers and gift to up hold our law you are free to go for your next mission."
Benjamin bows his head and leaves the court rooms and leaves the council. He feels ashamed, the robot understood the way Benjamin was feeling and comforts him knowing that they would have to come back soon.
Benjamin had caught on he knew by the way he was being questioned that it was a game in their eyes a game that Benjamin was willing to play which they did not know, Benjamin from that point would trust nobody. Even though Benjamin wanted to shout at anything and everything through the pressure of the court room he broke when he got to his quarters.
It seemed to Benjamin that everything had revised, he did not know whether it was there game or whether it was his mind. The death of the mayor was defiantly being playing on his mind and playing on his consciousness. The whole journey through the council all the questions after questions after questions it was like being a Ginny pig. There was something going on upstairs not upstairs in my mind but in theirs. Benjamin knew that there was something up, but he chose to ignore it that was Benjamin to a tee. It was like him to ignore his problems if they insisted and would wait for them to pilfered up and deal with

them later. He chose to ignore them for now. It was like the reversed had happened Benjamin was busy putting his thoughts beside with ease they meant nothing for now. All he wanted was a beer and a smoke. There was a knock at my quarters doors Benjamin did not want to answer it. but it was instinct that made him walk to the door. Benjamin opens the door, to his surprise it was personal. A conversation started. And there was an officer with him.
PERSONAL:" Hello."
BENJAMIN:" Hello, come in."
OFFICER: "We have been asked to give you this."
It was a badge the same badge that I was wearing on my suit it was the same badge that I was being offered to my robot we were going back to court this time my robot was on trial for an award.
COUNTCILLOR ANDREW: "Well it seems to me that you have done all you could have done to except and obey your orders you also are ready and free to go to your next mission."
"You are free to go."
The officer hand s Benjamin his next mission in an envelope in the envelope was his orders Benjamin thanks the officer for nothing and sends him on his way. Benjamin waits until the officer is at a distant and then opens the envelope in private but does not look at it. He closes the room door so that he has privacy.
In the envelope was the next job he looks at it hard thinking about what is in it. he takes she eve elope and puts it down on a table in the room, close to his bunk. It was a message from the court hearing this afternoon well that's what he thought. Benjamin was clearly in a bed mood a few minutes later senator Simon was to call upon him.
CENETOR SIMON: "Benjamin are you okay."
BENJAMIN: "Yeah I'm fine, just a little out of touch now due to the hearing, it has not sunk in just yet."
CENETOR SIMON:" It's not just the killing it's a mission you're the very best, probably the best in our world. You know already that you have been chosen to help their world to help mankind there are a lot of misguided people out there in our system. You nerve being employed to stop them do you understand."
BENAJMIN: I'm not sure that I do understand after the hearing today one second I'm doing right the next I'm doing wrong.
SENETOR SIMON:" You do not have to feel that way." What you are feeling Benjamin is the reverse it is like everything that you have ever experience after a battle it is the opposite experience of e=what you are

thinking, what you feel, what you see. it might take you a few days to understand it so get some rest".

Benjamin did not know what exactly the senator Simon was saying and again it seemed that their whole programme was the reverse of what benjamin was saying and thinking. Everything that I said to the council had reflected on him, it was very personal. There was a lot of pressure, but rule s were rules. And the whole court room seemed to be on the mayor's side. I was doing them a favour and it was like they were trying to twist everything I said at that point. Something was wrong not just in our council but on the planet. I did not find time to find the answer or the knowledge to understand it at this point, so I put it aside. I decided to play their game until I had more of an insight of what was going on and what I really wanted I was thinking that I was being used the thought was now that I was the target and I was going to be the hunted.

It was early morning after a good night of no sleep as I tossed and turned on my bunk half a wake and half asleep as I was heading out of my mind for some proper sleep I knew deep down that I was not going to get the rest I needed, and I knew that the only rest that I knew that I was going to get was on my own ship. As I adjusted my pillow over ten times within an hour, but I was still uncomfortable and at eased but in the end, I gave up I had to do something, and it was a smoke a cigarette. As I pushed it into my mouth and breathed the smoke out into the fresh air. I felt a little better, but I knew also that the feeling would not last, I needed to get away, but I had a contract to full fill. As I opened the eve elope there was three hundred thousand credits in it in space terms that's a lot of loot unfortunately for me it was a dream as I was asleep in the real envelope was the second job the second hit the man that I was going to kill. The next man was a priest a holy man what he had done I do not know I was not in the business of hanging around business that was not my business. His name was father frank I began to look at his profile early it said everything in the document in the envelope I had taken the letter out of its envelope.

I was back in the space ship this priest according to the court was being totally out of terms with his own spiritually by pushing the things that he preached was causing our planet and his world in to chaos. He had to be stopped, he was known to over express himself and sucking the life out of the people that wanted to understand but did not understand. I guess in a sense that he had gone a little over the top. It could have been a little nicer. Anyway, I Had a job to do and I had got compile to the letter what was in the envelope. I was heading back to the planet earth again.

The only problem this time was as it was calculated as I sat in the space chair in my cockpit. As I zoomed through the earth's atmosphere with my robot taking the control of the ship as I went to lie down and its crazy sunflowers for company we were going to make a hit in the day time. When I awoke I spoke to mar arty he gave me the priests exact coordinates as we landed just outside his church. I felt uneasy something was wrong. I went to my computer.

BENJAMIN: "Hay, computer you hailed me. What's up".
COMPUTER: "You seem to have a rival as there is already a hit on this man".
BENJAMIN: "What does this mean".
COMPUTER: We have two options, one you can full fill your orders and kill the priest or two you could kill the priest and then kill the hitman".
BENJAMIN: "What would be the outcome if I killed them both".
COMPUTER: "Good question I will have an answer for you in a second I am just going to send a message home".
Benjamin waits a few minutes on his toes in trepidation. The computer gives Benjamin an answer he tells Benjamin that he has permission to remove both if he can the hitman and now the priest were both going to die.

BENJAMIN:" Good."

Benjamin walks out of his space ship there are holy people everywhere, he knows he cannot touch them as they were who they were. He reaches into his pushing a button to close the visor down, so he is masked. Just as he nears his victim two motor bukes near him he finds the second hit the man on the motor cycle lifts his gun Benjamin can see it quite clearly. The man on the bike lifts his gun and fires maybe a round or two Benjamin attempts to take them out he lifts his gun and sends an array of bullets hitting the motor cycle at first them of Couse hitting the rider with nobody to control the bike the assign on the back was all left for dead as the bike crashes in as few on coming verses. There was a burst of flames but however Benjamin did not have enough time to go after them or even see if they alive or dead his real target now was the priest and after everything that just happened it made things a little easier as now there were just people watching the blaze of fire and smoke. Benjamin continues to walk into the building there are some guards by the targets doors before he can reach the priest he will have to remove the guards. The guards pick up Benjamin extremely fast they both came at him at once. It did not make things any easier as some of the crowd was now beginning to disperse Benjamin uses his helmet to get a picture of the priested helmet was computerised it locks on to his target Benjamin takes out the targets one by one until there was nobody left to guard the priest.

The priest did not see Benjamin coming, as he stood in the room full of his dead body guards he falls to his knees. Benjamin see no remorse. He pulls his gun out of his space suit.

BENJAMIN: "Any last requests."

The priest does not answer as Benjamin raises his arm. The priest is dead Benjamin's job for now is done the second target on his list has been assisted. Benjamin had put a few bullets through his head. He leaves the building calmly walking past people until he gets outside and calls upon his robot to send the space ship. As his ship arrives the cops turn up just a minute behind him that would be the oxygen and the hitman. Benjamin has no more time to play games.

Benjamin is in his cockpit making a getaway while he takes his space ship up more and more coppers are turning up.

As Benjamin is safely back on board the spirit, he has time to figure out the power of his badge he was not looking to confident. Benjamin tells his computer to go to stealth, as soon as the ship does Benjamin is out of there site of the authority's, he makes his escape.

The two cops were sitting just outside of the building while his cars computer is organizing the lock down of the area, so they can start the forensic proceedings. Just on the edge deciding if they should enter the scene of the crime they had no business there at that point as another team beat them to it. they discussed it for a minute or two. Between them and their boss who was on the end of the phone they both were being told no. they decide to go in to the building despite what they were told.
THE HITMAN: "Let's go in."
THE OXYGEN: I" do not know what I am doing I do think that this is a good idea."
THE HITMAN:" come on it will be an adventure. You might learn something."
THE OXYGEN: "We are going to be taken by the scuffs of our colours I bet I lose my badge. I will blame you."

The two cops both get out of the cool one they call it the cool one because it's on its number plates.
They enter the reception as the forensic team are looking at things and trying to figure it out. The two-start looking at things two until they bump in the three-opposing team and told to leave the scene there was a small conversation to go with the orders.
Benjamin was on his way back home to tell his council that the job had been done.
Back in the office block the two cops are hailed back to the scene and are welcomed to have a look around. The local authorities did not want the cops there, any of them. they were part of the evidence and were going to be questioned.
CHIEF: "Okay what are you too boys doing out of your jurisdiction."
The two cops did not answer they both knew that if they gave such as a twitch the chief would kick off and shout at them extremely loud.
They did not want to tell the chief that they were looking for a space ship and an alien got go with it.
They did not want to tell him that they were slowly hunting a space killing hitman.
THE HITMAN: "Look it is just following portico were just gathering a few facts."
THE OXYGEN:" we were down stairs in the area, in the car we heard gun fire."

CHIEF: "do you expect me to believe that did you to know that you could be arrested for a breech interfering with police business."
THE HITMAN:" I think we should tell him"

THE OXYGEN:" No I do not the guys crazy let's get out of here,

honestly do we look like the police yeah I think so what could he not

see."

The two cops decide to walk out.

They both leave the scene heading back to the verse the cool one.
THE OXYGEN: "That was close a little bit too close for my likening. Come on get in what I did not like is what I just saw it is the kind of mess that you can never get out of your head. Do I get paid for that because if I do I'm going to ask for a pay rise?"
THE HITMAN: "Probably not but we could ask."
Benjamin is back in space or there about, he knows that he's got away with it. The first and now the second he sends us a message to his planet telling the council that the second job is done. He gets no reply. Knowing that his council had got the message he thinks that he is being respected and they were letting rest.
Benjamin closes his eye's the thought of killing did not leave a great impression on the mind. He was trying to find the save in his head because it was a recurring thought and that was the problem. But however, he knew the feeling would subside but right now he was mourning.

Benjamin closes his eyes again, he knows that he is safe but how safe was the question? after the work is done who knows what Benjamin future will be. After an hour or so he opens his eyes the voice of a friend his robot mar arty wakes him.
MARARTY: "Welcome back."
BENJAMIN: "Thank you that was a seriously rough ride, where are we."
MARARTY: "Are you okay."
BENJAMIN: "Yes I am."
MARARTY:" Did you use the badge."
BENJAMIN: "I cannot remember."
Benjamin tries to account but his mind is blank. He thinks even harder until he receives it he continues yes, I remember I was a tiger and I clawed some guy to death.
MARARTY: "Close, you shot him."
BENJAMIN: "That does not make me feel any better."
MARARTY: "You chose to remember, you did not have to."
Well I guess the badge works.

MARARATY: "Do you know what the rest does."
BENJAMIN: "No I have not had the chance to use it yet."
MARARTY:" Would you like me to help you understand it."
BENJAMIN: "Not right now we can do it another time. I need to recover I need to wake up maybe later."
As Benjamin closes his eyes again he drifts off again. Mar arty agrees he should be resting. And tells him to go back to sleep. As Benjamin as Benjamin slowly falls asleep he's dreaming of his next hit. This time it was the mayor of New York. As he dreams as in any dream before he awakes and misses the outcome he must improvise. He knows part of the future this time he awakes suddenly with the sweat to go with it, falling off his bed on to the floor and stays there still half confused award half conscious and still half asleep.

Mar arty turns the gravity on using it slowly to lift Benjamin back on his bunk as his body slowly rises upwards floating the robot slowly pushes him back on to the bunk and straps him down. Mara arty puts some music on he's into classical. His two other friends the two sunflowers are still asleep also the robot is left alone while playing the music he is talking the computer to keep himself entertained. While the robot is looking after the space ship. While everybody is asleep the robot decides if he should take the space back down to planet earth. He decides that he would wait for Benjamin to awake instead. The robot was scared for Benjamin he was the robots best friend the robot watches the two sun flowers they had awoke by the music and had started to sing along with it. cheering the robot out of its worries. The robot sets up the coordinates to take Benjamin back to his home planet.as the sun flowers were in the back-ground singing soul lyrics to classical music mar arty joins in the flowers were fun to be with once you had got to know them. As mar arty sings with the sun flowers Benjamín slowly awakes finally feeling like his old self but in a temper, that was the price you pay for killing. He did not know what was to come he did not know that being a killer was a disease. As he undoes the straps that have him locked down he floats gently around to his cockpit
Checking messages and making sure that they were not being followed. As the earth did not have the technology to follow Benjamín waits in silence now for the next orders of the destination of his next target will be they were off to New York in a few days.
Two days had past and Benjamín had received nothing he wanted to go back to the earth there was something about that planet that he was drawn to. Benjamin closes his eyes but only for a moment he was thinking why does the silhouette want to destroy this planet

May be Benjamín thinks as he enters his dream.

Benjamin dreams of the planet earth things start to look dark at first. He was dreaming of peace but for some strange reason that he does not know, things take a shape and things take change. Add the dream becomes darkness. There's destruction and then Benjamín suddenly awakes, not knowing what the dream was about Benjamín wants to go back to the earth as he was in love way=the what he saw in his dreams. He turns to his robot mar arty.
BENJAMIN: "Bring me some pitchers of the planet earth."
MARARTY: "The planet earth."
BENJAMIN: "Yes."
Mar arty turn to a big screen basically the ships ships cockpit window and asks Benjamín again just to make sure what he wants.
It seems to Benjamín with the knowledge in front of him that the earth is smaller than the moon and even smaller the sun and even smaller the Benjamin's home planet.
MARARTY: "The earth is still a big place."

Even so the planet earth had been abused by humans Benjamín plugs himself in to the robot and then in to the computer on his deck side dashboard. Benjamin down loads all the knowledge of the planet to himself. Mar arty does and within twelve hours Benjamín has all the knowledge of the earth that man has recorded to date. When he has finished he does not know that he has overloaded his brain with the knowledge. Being an alien and not human he passes out, but he now knows everything while he sleeps. As he sleeps the knowledge of the earth rips through him with even its future he falls father into a deeper sleep. and has uncontrollable fits as his brain fights the power of it. the knowledge and the power of was taking over Benjamín as he falls even in to a deeper sleep.

His robot is confused and is worried about Benjamín he had not woken yet, and it had been a few days the two flowers plants were put close to him they might annoy him back from where ever he was. They were all ways being noisy it was just an idea. But it was a good idea at the time although it did not work.
FLOWER 1: "Do you think that he will awake."
FLOWER 2:" he will come around eventually."
FLOWER 1: "he has been life less for days."
FLOWER 2:" two days."
FLOWER 1: "let's sing a song it might help. Like some soul music."
FLOWER 2: "I do not think that will work but we can try."
The flower s burst in a song and there dancing and shouting in hope that Benjamín come back he does not wake up.
Benjamin is still in the deep sleep dreaming but this time he is dreaming od =f the next hit which meant that he was on his way back. When Benjamín awake all, he could say was the words." Bad people come first."

Mar arty thinks that the badge is to power full for Benjamin to weld and tries to remove it in hope that he would wake up but the badge un known to the robot will never come off. Every time he does try the badge grows stronger. The power was also within Benjamin, mar arty is confused Benjamin knows. The two cops in the cool one is also thinking about Benjamin the deep sleep that Benjamin was blocking their thoughts the power off the sound of Benjamin in his sleep was dealing for both cops as they both clasps their head in pain that the sound was so powerful windows in buildings that Benjamin had been in would crack an explode. As Benjamin slowly dreams he his arm slowly move s up to his chest and he presses the badge unconsciously. On this occasion nothing happens the robot is concerned as his actions are simultaneous he had done these two or three times within a couple of hours. Benjamin cannot stop repeating the term spirit. Huis happen every hour in to the morning the robot=get thinks that the job is to tough and wants Benjamín to bow out. But he has no way of telling him. The robot has run out of ideas and goes for a recharge.

CHAPTER FOUR
MOVIE BREAKDOWN

When Benjamín finally woke up it was like the end of the movie, tears from everybody including the welcoming by the flowers. It was amazing how much his three companions cared and how much the sleep effects Benjamin's mind. With a moment Benjamín whole personality changed. He moved differently and spoke differently, it was obvious there was a change in his whole personality there was something new about him. Mar arty took a second to think that it was cool Benjamín had not noticed it as much as his friends on the spaceship. The flowers did not even notice, and they notice everything, they caught on in the end. In all the confusion Benjamín was also receiving his orders and was glad that he would be returning to the planet earth. He seemed to think that it was a good place to be his friend s thought differently.
Benjamin: "let's go to New York."
Mar arty: "I'm just plugging in the coordinates now. We have one hour and two minutes hyper speed
Benjamin was on his seconded hit the mayor of New York city this hit was going to be different Benjamín had to go into his office he had not planned how he was going to kill the man just yet. At that point he did not even know where New York was or how he was going to do it.
The two cops in the cool one had been tipped off somehow, they were at the scene as Benjamín lands his space ship it did worried Benjamín as such, but the less people know that Benjamin's on the planet the better and easier it was for him to do his job. Benjamin also knows that he has the cops watching him as he lands the vesicle he turns his stealth on nobody can see him on top of the building he sits and waits the cops were thinking where the hit was going to be they believed that it was going to be outside but in fact it was inside that was Benjamin's plan.
The front of the building was guarded who ever tipped them of gave them the wrong information. As the mayor was speaking his last words in his speech he was waiting to receive a bullet, but nothing happened he was guarded but guarded with the wrong information.

shoulder, but not bad as the bullet that was meant for him hits his badge forcing it to half malfunction as he starts to flicker as Benjamín waits via award with his robot who tells him to wait it was not damaged but will take a minute to reboot Benjamín reply to that is that he has not got a minute and tries to explain that he is on the mayors door step. Benjamin is in luck he manages to take four more guards out skill fully as his suit boots up. The first one takes it in the legs Benjamín walks past him kicking his weapon aside the only reason that Benjamin shot him in the legs was that he did not like killing the innocent. Still injured and in pain he kneels down one knee and send another one down shooting him thrugh the chest one of the guards hides Benjamin was aware as the forth trees to board the helicopter but is thrown off Benjamín was in fixated he did not even notice the helicopter he hits is badge again it malfunctions has in full view of what was left they could now see him, he takes another bullet this time it is in his leg the top of his thigh as he is down on one knee again he take us the chance leaving the mayor and focusing on the helicopter. He looks real hard and sets his sight on the tail then mar arty tips him and tells him to go for the engine he sets himself up a line of fire and then take she shoot missing the first time and blowing the helicopter clean out of the sky on the second. The mayor is on the floor with debris and machine parts in small fire Benjamín slowly walks towards him the mayor is pleading to him.

THE MAYOR:" Wait, we can make a deal."

BENJAMIN: "There is no deal."

The mayor stands s up on his feet Benjamín know that his court means business and do not make deals. The mayor stubble s backward s still pleading.

MAYOR: "look, look."

That's where it ended Benjamín grabs the mayor pushing backwards until he is on the edge with one more push it was enough to make him slip backwards over the edge of the wall. The mayor had fallen to his death.

Benjamin walks back to his ship just as he is boarding the cops turn up. Benjamin is safe the cops see nothing and Benjamín is off in the cockpit tapping the coordinates of getting his ship back in to space. The two cops are trying to figure out the mess that Benjamín left behind him.

OXYGEN:" What the hell is that."

HITMAN:" I do not know."

Expecting to take a bullet with his bullet proof vest on and all his men what he was told did not happen in a way he was relieved that it did not happen. After a speech which ended we words of something like let's make America a great place and love one another and a load of lovely dove stuff like let's do good to all people, he leaves his testimony with his public. He leaves as he make is way of the stage and down on the concrete floor and back in the large hotel behind him and makes it upstairs s right to the top of the building, there is a helicopter waiting for him.
Benjamin is watching the whole thing he see his future and makes a hit on the mayor he also sees himself escaping he is happy that he sees himself get away. what's to come next was not nice especially if you could visualize it. As the mayor is hassled upstairs Benjamín makes his move he steps out of his craft still in touch with his ship through an ear piece straight to his cockpit to the robot and the space ship they were told to meet him half way. The robot miss calculates as the mayor's team move faster than Benjamín had expected they were moving to the top of the building fast. Benjamin must think and be quick about it.
Although he aware he hits his badge not once but twice giving him the power of invisibility. He raises his arm catching up with the guards just as they reach the top of the building and were entering the big H on the helicopter pad as the helicopter lands Benjamín take is the first shot hitting the guard in the shoulder leaving him on the hard-concrete floor bleeding. When the other guard s turn to return fire there's nobody there they did not have a clue Benjamín fires again taking out a second one, they return fire again but this time it is Benjamín that is on the receiving end of things as he is injured and is hit in the

OXYGEN:" I do not think the chief will be happy."
HITMAN:" Get him on the phone."
OXYGEN:" No, but whatever it was it was moving fast. I'm going to call it in."
HITMAN: "This is the cool one to the club we have a UFO Flying over New York can you pick it up copy."
The cops get the reply and the air force is scrambled. Within a few minutes of that phone call Benjamín s robot receive a message that tells Benjamín that his craft had been spotted and now is being followed.
ROBOT:" We are being followed."
BENJAMIN: "followed by what."
ROBOT: "it looks to me to be a fighter jet according to the computer systems there coming in fast."
BENJAMIN: "Try our cloaking devices"
ROBOT: "I have tried there to close."
BENJAMIN:" okay take us up in to the ozone layer the air will be too cold for them to breathe."
ROBOT:" Okay."
The pilot loses Benjamín and his space ship up above the clouds and his theory seemed to work the pilot radios it in
PILOT: "This is voodoo the unidentified object has disappeared I cannot see him anywhere and I have lost him on my radar. I'm coming home."

CHAPTER FIVE
SILHOUETTE

The man that Benjamín is worried about was another assassin called the silhouette he was the only other space being that could have a chance of destroying Benjamín and he could probably destroy the space council. Benjamin knew that they were scared too. They had met on many occasions several infect Benjamín failed to beat him in combat. Also, Benjamin knew that they were rivals. And had to keep looking over his shoulder Benjamín knew how good the silhouette was. Benjamin knew that one day he would look over his shoulder and he would be there. It was the kind of fright that would keep you awake at night.

The silhouette was watching Benjamín very carefully the silhouette had just as many tricks up his sleeve as Benjamín.

The power that he had were like Benjamin's badge infect the silhouette was ten times more powerful which made him ten times harder. The silhouette did not have a spaceship. Even though he resembled a human form he could fly through space pallet to planet without breathing and he could move just as fast as Benjamin's space ship if not probably faster.

The silhouette was at his council the council were discoing Benjamín without his permission and with him not being there. The silhouette was trying to claim that Benjamín was a bad seed and was asking them permission to destroy him. They were going got double cross him as they were slowly begging to believe the silhouette there was a long conversation a head of them the council begin again with a simple question?
COUNTCILOR: "Why are you here."
SILHOUETTE: "To serve you my lords."

COUNTCILOR:" There is a great in balance in your world and you believe that it is Benjamín, am I right."
COUNTCILOR:" is that all you believe."
SILHOUETTE:" If you do not send me to him there will be mass destruction our planets will collide with the human world and planet earth. People will die."
COUNTCILOR:" what powers do you weld."
SILHOUETTE:" I am here to server you all."
COUNTCILOR: "answer the question what powers do you weld."
SILHOUETTE: "Your power."
COUNTCILOR: "Yes your power."
SILHOUETTE: "You do my lords."
COUNTCILOR: "That is all for now on no account are you to approach Benjamín on this occasion."
SILHOUETTE: "Benjamin is a traitor and he deserves to die,"

The silhouette continues.
SILHOUETTE: "Are you blind, is your government so blind they cannot see."
COUNTCILOR: "Hold your tongue, you are dismissed from the council the meeting is over."
The silhouette bows his head and walks out of the court room the councillor's then close the meeting. There is an army of silence as they discuss what they had just heard in the meeting from in the meeting room the council can hear the shouts in anger of the silhouette from inside of the room. The silhouette ws angry over the decision he was smashing things up Ans giving the guards a fight.

COUNCILOR: Do you think he is upset
COUNCILOR: "just a little, however we can just wright Benjamín off he has, or should I say doing his job. There's a lot riding on him and on the planet earth I believe it is doomed killing Benjamín will not help it, your own child, he is like a son to all of us."
After all the noise the silhouette had finally calmed down the councillors walk out still talking.

CHAPTER SIX
TECHNICAL MALFUNCTION

Benjamin was busy fixing the ship it was one problem to the other as he floats around the room pulling leads out and replacing them, cutting wires and hoping that he was doing the job right, he calls for assistants, but his robot did not hear him meaning that he also had a problem with the robot's communication systems. Benjamin uses a walkie take but the same again he gets no answer.
Second time around he chooses to do it the human way and give us a shout. There's is still no answer. After waiting a few minutes or so he gives up he floats off to find it, the robot is in his cockpit seat, the floe=wars are busy talking which normally meant that something was

up, and they normally only talk when Benjamín is around. Other than that, they were mostly silence.

BENJAMIN: "Are you okay mar arty."

There is no answer, as he finds s him he lifts him over on to his back. As he had been working on some of the ships electric she already had the screw driver in his hands he pulls it out of his pocket, Benjamin puts the screw driver into the robot's circuits. There were a few sparks nothing serious but knowing that he might have made a technical malfunction worse.

The robot still does not comply, and Benjamin is at a loss, he might have to return to his home planet and have the robot replaced.

Benjamin has other priority the next target the next hit, as he closes his eyes he can clearly everything he knows that he is close he decides to leave the robots side and think of things by himself. He leaves the robot to fix its self, it was built that way. It was never too late that is what Benjamin was thinking about the next victim. As Benjamin sits in the cockpit he is visualizing the plan of how he was going to introduce himself to his next victim.

Meanwhile the oxygen and the hitman are trying to figure out who is Benjamín and why he is on the planet. And why he is killing people they are left thinking about the two murders. It seems to everybody that Benjamín is not the nice guy who he seemed to be, yet. As Benjamín is above the ozone layer planning the next job, the next move, the next hit, as Benjamín meditates through his mind he sees everything but not just his escape which h leaves him a little confused and not believing it his next victim the profile an actor. The computer up loads his file s and name. Benjamín get the information quickly and wants to move fast. There was something funny about this hit, it did not seem right. In any case he was up for it.

Benjamin was quizzed by the next hit it was a librarian, Benjamín was thinking why? and what? As he had thought that librarians were peaceful people and enjoyed being in silence. Some one upstairs seemed to think deferent, Benjamín did not believe it. Benjamín checks the time obviously he was late. And the assassin must be on time. He callas for his robot mar arty. forgetting that he was out of order and fixing himself at that time he turns to his computer, as he pulls the robot out of the seat and dumps him on the floor next to the sun flowers hoping that he would come around and that the point the sunflowers are singing to bring him back. Luckily the robot had set the coordinates to the planet earth before he had malfunctioned. Benjamin was heading straight for trouble as he zoomed by the robot's coordination he was taking Benjamín away from then planet but that was not want Benjamín wants he has a hit to make and need is to be on the earth the robot was presiding the opposite. It took Benjamin an hour to reperceive with his robot, out he did it by his computer within an hour Benjamín is back up above the earth in the ozone. Hoping that he had not been spotted by British aerospace and knowing that he not being detected. There was nothing on his mind harder. Benjamin wants his old pal the robot mar arty back, two brains are better than one. Benjamin's thinks hard it would be easier as Benjamin now must control the assassination of the third target, while controlling everything in the ship as well as making plans for the target removal. Benjamin thinks it is going to be easy, how wrong he was.

But in fact, it was harder than he thought, it was the opposite Benjamín had followed the librarian by foot straight from his space craft, he was lead to a train station, Benjamin watches in silence. Benjamin realizes that the journey that he was being taking on was too long and he had no time to make an assassination. He was worried that he would be seen making the attempt on that life.

He sends a message to his friend the robot, in the message in a message the message had an address in it. knowing that just recently that the robot had mal functioned and hoping that he had got over it whatever the problem was. Benjamin not forgetting the target and follows him, then the Liberian his journey home was probably his last. Benjamin wants to get close, close enough to lift his wallet. But still there was to many people around the target and him. Benjamin canno0t get a clear shot and the crowds are working on the targets behalf. Benjamin calls to his space ship for assistants, while losing his target for the second time.

The robot is awake and complies to Benjamin's orders. Benjamin gets a good look at the targets face

Benjamin knows that he was close enough to make the hit, if it was only for the crowd being in the way but as he counts it could have been a good thing, but without the right back up things might get a little out of hand. Things might or could go wrong, he was to wait. As he waits for information on the characters identification, it was only a minute before Benjamín had a match. The hair the colour of his eyes and even more so. Benjamin raises his weaponeer. Benjamin believe that he has found the target, he lifts his arm and puts more than a few bullets into the target. Benjamin does not think about it straight away, but he must have put at least half a magazine of bullets into him. What was worrying Benjamin was that it was right in front of the public, that's not good publicity as if I needed it. Benjamin was hoping and thinking that the people were too busy to notice so it was put aside or maybe they were trying to scare as him. It was san orchard situation and even more complicated to explain.

As the librarians was dead and Benjamin was left holding his body as he catches him him just before he hits the floor making sure that he is dead not wanting to but must listen to his last6 requests Benjamín lets him die showing no remorse at all.

The hit was made in a train station and there were many people about and as there was many people around it looks like Benjamín may have got away with it as the people were into minding their own business. Benjamin was able and was clever enough to make the dead target look like dummies leaving him there with a paper on the station bench. As Benjamín waits for a moment to finish him off completely and eliminate his problem he calls for his space ship to come and find him. He calls for his space ship to come and find him, so he can make a getaway.

Benjamin plans on this occasion where to turn to the public he has a problem even though he tried to introduce himself the public were not happy Benjamín in all his angst opened fire killing an old lady who ws throwing herself about, another lady was blaming him for the death of her friend. Another lie. Benjamin's approach to the earth qasr not as welcoming as he would of thought. It sent shockwaves through the entire nation, Benjamín was now all over the news. As Benjamín tried to make it back to his spaceship the crowd was trying to over throw him. His spaceship sat the end of the plat form, as he pushed his way through the commuters and finally escaping he coolly looks at the destruction that he has left behind once aboard the ship the oxygen and his partner the hitman urn up they were not too far behind him.

Benjamin stops before he enters his ship, he stands their just outside the ships bay doors and takes a good look at the carnage that he had made. As he turns as he walks on to the ships deck it is like nothing had happened. He hears a familiar voice the oxygen and then the hitman as they push past the body's that Benjamín had left behind and alive they all had a different story about the hit making it difficult for the two cops to work things out.

Benjamin is thinking that he was lucky to escape, he makes his way back through threw his ship to his cockpit. Benjamin starts a conversation with his robot and computer.

BENAJMIN: "Full thrusters, take me up."

There was no reply but within a minute the computer recognised the order and with a few seconds Benjamín was out of danger and up into the stars. He was back hoovering in and around the ozone, amongst the planets skis.

Benjamin is content knowing that he is safe again as he sits in his chair the two-sun flower sari talking giving Benjamín a lift. Benjamin again falls in to a deep sleep as he is dreaming only a few minutes before he wakes however this are not normal dreams he sees things and hears things he believes that he is dreaming of his or the future.

In the end Benjamin disregards, it was a nightmare and thinks of his home planet he did not know at the time that they were going to double cross him.

Although all the dreams he was having also left a message an exact message and he knew that the silhouette had been watching him there was a positive change in Benjamín s behaviour. As now he knows that he is being watched or followed. Benjamin wakes as the sun rises it looks like it is going to be a long day, Benjamin calls for his robot and looks around for him. The robot was out cold it looks like he had t=run out of energy again Benjamín sails=as he knew that he had been entertain9ng the f=sun flowers. It was too much excitement.

CHAPTER SEVEN
IT IS ALL IN THE WRIST

Benjamin has some time to spare as he is slowly putting his crimes behind him, as he waits for instructions for the next hit. Benjamin needs to find somewhere to practice and learn the skills of the badge. As Benjamín has some time to spare he slowly puts his past of his recent future behind him, as he waits for his next instructions of his next hit. Benjamin needs to find some where he can practice his badge, as Benjamín make sure his arrival to the planet earth is nice and safe, he was looking for some nice land in an area that had not been used. Something derelict or even something hidden out of the way Something on open ground, somewhere he can cloak his ship and not be found.

As he makes his way back to the planet earth he speaks to his computer the computer says to Benjamín that there is no =where and there was nothing on the computer=zed map that would give them the time or space to land. Benjamin orders the ship to land. The computer still denies the ship to land in the end Benjamín tells his computer to find a forest and then continues to ask him if it is a safe place to land his vasal .M array butts in and a whole new discussion begins, in the end Benjamín is right the forest was the right place to Lanes=d Benjamín computer seemed to think differently and the robot had his opinion. Benjamín asks his computer to give him a computerized map of the land that they were in. Benjamín has no choice but to sit in the forest. He lands s his space ship in the trees amongst the forest brown and green.

As Benjamín stands outside of his space ship in the forest, the freshness of the air hits him straight away, this was a lot different from the city, Benjamin wants to change his clothe s as he trees to take off his suit, he struggles as the badge would not let him and he is left as he had started in a suit that he cannot remove. Benjamin finally catches on. As Benjamín plays around with the suit trying to figure it out mar arty finally wakes up and joins Benjamín. Benjamín is outside and has his back to his ship the robot was extending his neck just to watch Benjamín and all the excitement. Benjamin presses his badge not once but three times turning him in to a tiger. The robot congratulated Benjamín. Benjamin calls out to the robot and says I'm going for a stroll. Benjamin was impressed with the badge, as he moved through the forest slowly. Benjamin did not know at that time that he could speak too, his mind was connected to the robot and the spaceships computer as they had started talking.

As Benjamín slowly move s through the forest getting used to be an animal he begins to enjoy the badge as he gets more and More confident he begins to feel it true power and begins to run.
BENJAMIN: "This is awesome I am a tiger."

And he is excited. Benjamin slowly6 gets the feel of the change from man to animal, he is beginning to enjoy the badge. As he is getting more and more comfortable and comp ident he begins to run,

ROBOT:" Your running."
BENJAMIN: "Not yet but I will be."
Benjamin starts to pick up the speed loving every minute of it as he picks up speed he smoothly doges in and out of the forest trees.
As he moves faster and faster, he was a couple of miles away from his space ship, he stops dead right on a small cliff edge. He does not have to use the badge to morph back he merely just has to think it. It takes him a good hour to figure it out. As Benjamín is at the tip of the edge of the small cliff top with the memories of the water fall which is in front of him to take away. Mar arty tells Benjamín where he is and tells him where is going wrong with the badge. He the robot is pupping the knowledge into Benjamín using his mind Benjamín manages to morph back to his half alien half human self. He catches on a within a moment Benjamín back being Benjamin, but only for a moment again he touches his badge and he is off again racing back to his space ship as the tiger. As he nears the destination of the space ship he morphs back to Benjamín he thinks that the badge is incredible and with all the excitement crawls tiredly back on to the ship. With the robot lowering the cargo bays doors as is now on his feet
Benjamin decides that he has had enough of the badge for one day and is eager to speak to the robot about it. As he tries to take his suit off he cannot, forgetting what he had been told that once the badge is on you it cannot be removed. Benjamin is confused but not upset until he gets into his cockpit seat.
The flowers are talking again and joking about Benjamín they laugh with smiles and eventually break into song. The robot awakes Benjamín what was there next destination. Benjamin subjects that they should stay put for now. He still must attempt another trail with the badge. Benjamin was counting that if it was possible for them to stay in the forest it seemed quiet and peaceful. However, Benjamin thinks it might not be such a good idea as there is always someone about.

Benjamin does not want the trouble, Benjamín calculates that is two more days before his suit will be ready for the next four tests. After a few days pass Benjamin is ready to make another attempt in the suit he was going to try and morph.
Benjamin stands outside his space ship again by his cargo doors he takes a deep breath the robot has Benjamin's back and extends his next as he watches Benjamín for a better look. Benjamin turns his head a little just getting a clamp of the robot.
BENJAMIN: "Are you ready."
MARARTY: "Ass you are."
Benjamin taps his badge not once, not twice but three times. He disappears for a minute like a hologram. Then he morphs and instead of being one of him there are three of him. Benjamin ask toward she image he knows already that he control them through his mind he vie them a commitment Benjamín again was amazed also because they could talk amounts themselves.

They were a little bit more than a hologram. Benjamin take she lead and tells the first one to reach for his phaser, it does then he tells it put the phaser down on the ground. It does so. Even though the first commandment went okay it was harder to use then the tiger and Benjamín knows that it will take a bit of time understanding this super power. As the day went on day turning into night. Benjamin is giving the last command of the evening which was to get the hologram to pick his reopened up off the floor, mere thought at that point was not working. The next morning Benjamín plays with them all day until he understands s the badges power and it was going to take Benjamín a little more than twenty-four hours to understand the whole badge and not just that the suit too.
Benjamin was concerned for time as he had been there for nearly three days Benjamín was slowly getting used to it, but it was coming slow. Benjamin is believing that there may be a problem a fault in the suit. Benjamin is left to think and find a solution. He comes up with one answer that the badge needs light to work to function at his best or it could be the other way around it needed darkness.

Benjamin continues to study the badge while the darkness that he needs is just coming as the darkness slowly approaches as the sun goes

down and disappears over the horizon. Benjamin now can test the badge and suit again.
This time he can feel the power of the forest he could seriously hear the animals of the night. As Benjamin prepares himself to go out into the darkness a full moon and he knew that the wolfs would out on their hunt although it did not darter him.

Benjamin did not want to venture far to the waterfall and back about four miles all in all. As the forest knew him but not knowing its actual powers he had known understood two of the badges powers. As the night went on the calling signs of the wolf packs could clearly be heard. All the other forest animal life seemed to be blocked out due to the wolfs cry. He continues to practice and a was right the suit seems to be powered from and through the darkness. But still worked in the daylight. It was now extremely powerful.
Benjamin was now looking down at his badge and feeling it's power almost straight away it seemed to Benjamín that is was a simple design it was like one of those school badges that you would wear on your blazer except it was like made of mental and it felt weightless. I kind of felt sorry for the person who created it. it ws extremely futuristic either way it was done the badge was on Benjamín.
After the evening work Benjamín makes it back to his ship and his feeling tired aware of still being in the forest he closes to sleep outside. He could taste the air it was a little bit better than the city's air.

Benjamin find as tree to rest against close but not too far from his space ship.

Benjamin falls asleep under the stars for the first time he does not wake up until the early hours of the morning he is awoken by his robot, it was not normal for the robot to leave his space ship but on this occasion, it was fine by Benjamín. The robot had seen something and wanted to explore he had seen a butterfly and wanted to chase it, the robot was welding g a butterfly net and Benjamín had to smile. He found the robots actions this morning rather amusing. The robot wanted a butterfly to study it was as clear as that the robot did not catch it to his own and Benjamín dismay, but Benjamín had to laugh. Benjamin continues throughout the morning practicing the morphing and finally figures it out save power number two complete. Once this was done Benjamín was feeling a little better. He moves to third, the third power that he welds is the power of defines a shield. As he taps his badge for the third time the badge leaves the suit but only for a second the human eye would not see it but Benjamín could. The badge becomes mechanical and fits into a hole in the lower part of the arm and grow extremely fast reappearing on the top of Benjamín left hand and reshaping It is getting large, large enough to become a shield. The shield is bullet proof Benjamín fins out he thinks that it is amazing. He calls out to his robot to come and have a look he was busy talking to the sunflowers Benjamín calls him again his telling him to bring his phaser. The robot finally walks out down the cargo bay. Once Benjamín had warmed himself up he shouts to the robot to take a few shots at him the robot was quizzed then catches on.

Benjamin asks the robot to stand till as he is experimenting with the power of the shield turning the shield off then on checking how quick it is. He was happy that it worked fast the robot remind s Benjamín that it might even work better in the dark. Benjamin thanks him for his input.
BENJAMIN: "Okay are you ready."

ROBOT: "ready."
BENJAMIN: "Go on fire."
The robot is hesitant as he cannot see the outcome.
BENJAMIN: "Come on take a shot."
Benjamin mind is working quickly unlocking the badge as it goes through its sequences. As the badge move s into his lower left arm he feels the power of it. the shield quickly appears Benjamín with his robot then practice for the =e rest of the day. Until the badge runs out of energy for that one programme. They must wait for the evening to recharge it.

The robot was loving it he would play with Benjamín and the suit for hours teaching Benjamín everything and his ship was just about working too. As Benjamín sits down on the cargo doors he is waiting for the sun to go down and recharge his suit. As the sun was going down it brought a little bit of peace and quiet as Benjamín was just finishing some minor repairs to his cockpit.
BENJAMIN:" I do not know why they have sent us here in this hunk of junk."

Benjamin is trying, and he is working hard as he moves s leads and sockets from his dash board and replaces the components. To fix the ship for a better performance for his next journey. He steps outside and asks his ship to cloak it does and then he uncloaks it. Benjamin is now feeling a little bit clever as now he can communicate with his space ship through voice. Benjamin is happy but concerned that he cannot wait for the night to come. And he is hesitant about deciding on whether they should leave the forest it might be too soon. Benjamin wants to test the ships speed, but it was to light at that moment and it obvious that he would been scene, and it would be stupid as he would have the authority breathing down his neck. He turns to his robot for a discussion the robot tells Benjamín to hack the air space via the computer and he will tell you wants up there in the skis above.
A few minutes pass and the computer tell Benjamín that there are too many planes up there and it would be dangerous, and they would be in a better position to wait for the night. Benjamin thinks as he tries to find another solution.

Just as Benjamín turns he hears a click there was somebody behind him
BENJAMIN: "Is that you mar arty."
There is no answer and Benjamín is puzzled. He calls out again.

BENJAMIN: "Is that you robot. Stop playing games and get on board."

There's another click even closer than the robot appears he pokes his head just inside the cock pit doors. then he appears to Benjamin's surprise with a visitor.

FARMER: "I have been watching you."

Benjamin knew that what he just said was impossible he would have picked it through his suit and computer. On that account Benjamín knew that he could not be trusted as the man continues.

FARMER:" Did you know that you are a wanted man. You and your space ship are all over the news."

Benjamin knew that it was another lie. Again, his robot would have told him via his computer as the robot once plugged in would have received the broadcast yes, the robot is that advanced he conceive things like messages through his systems that he does not even have to watch.

FARMER: "There is a bounty on your head."

Again, the farmer had told a lie there was no such thing. As the farmer makes himself welcome on the space ship the farmer pushes Benjamín hard enough to knock him into his dash board as the man does Benjamín lands on some button closing the space ship cargo doors the only way in and the only way out. Benjamin has just enough time to press his badge he changes in to the tiger Benjamin takes a swipe at the man knocking the gun that he is holding out of his hands and taking a second swipe knocking the man down as the farmer craws looking for a way out, Benjamín slowly walks towards him pushing his noise and face down upon him Benjamín s says to him that he better leaves before he gets hungry. Benjamin swipes at the farmer leaving him with a scratched face to remember him by. He changed back to Benjamín and opens the cargo doors.

Benjamin continues as the man had only just got on his feet Benjamín continuers that the stretch on his face is for him to remember the day. The farmer gets to run, he goes back into the forest Benjamín find s his weapon and breaks it into tow and throws it into some stubs after he takes the cartridges out he keeps in for a souvenir.

Benjamin did not believe that the man would say anything he was to scare but Benjamín had to make sure and heads straight to his cockpit while he was speaking to his robot thanking him for the backup then shouting at him for letting the man onto his ship.

BENJAMIN: I want all the diagnostics on that man find smutch and pull up his file and file everything that you have just witnessed as from then, when you first met the man.

The robot does as it is told. Benjamin continues with his reaction not sure how he is taken it. he continues to his computer he also tells the computer to check a run on the farmers file. The robots call Benjamín over to him he shows him that the ships cameras on the outside have a recording of it. Benjamín feels an ease.

Benjamin wants a close of the man who claimed he was the bounty hunter Benjamín does not know yet but in the future, he will have one. The robot pulls a picture up on to the cockpit screen.

He is there. Benjamin can now get a better look. Benjamin believes that he will come back probably not on his own. Benjamin cloaks his ship and as he said the farmer came back but this time not ion his own but with a poise. Benjamin was aware of this. Benjamin ship was fully cloaked the only way of them finding it was if they bumped in to it. Benjamín had full view of what was going outside the ship as he was watching via the spaceships cameras. The man was begging to look stupid as the rest of the poise were calling him crazy band other things the man was still content to try and explain. The incident went no farther as the poise gave up and went home. the man's last words where I swear he was hear,

The man was now on his own and Benjamín was thinking of killing him, lucky for the man that Benjamín was level headed and knows by protocol that he cannot just kill any one there had to be another reason and beaming did not have it. so, he lets the man go even though he seen the inside of the ship.

Also, he could only use the badge in self-defence. Benjamin is called the computer the computer tells Benjamín that their game is not over the mean had come back this time with dogs. And they were picking up Benjamín sense Benjamin was slowly bottling himself up.
Benjamin grips his seat with excitement he was one hoping that they would find him. Just one it would take just one of them to bump into the ship and a battle would begin. Not that the human weapons were powerful enough to do any damage they did not know that besides it would give Benjamín something to do. After around fifteen of standing around talking and scuffles this framer was being taken for a fool his friends walk off again. Benjamin knows that he is running out of time and must find another plan=cue to dwell u8ntill his next target. Ads another place to study the rest of the badge. Within a second Benjamin receives a message.
BENJAMIN: "Buckle up were getting out of here."
ROBOT: "Where are we going."
BENJAMIN: "I do not know yet, but my target is at home."

CHAPTER EIGHT
THE TIP OFF

The next target was not going to be easy. This time it was the head of the police force why I asked the question well he was the court man in the city. Benjamin has all his details on file in front of him. Hr=e continues stop read Benjamin tries to laugh this one off Benjamín space craft's position was just below the ozone. He always starts the tasks that he has from there and strategizes his plans. He spends a hole day just watching the targets last moves according to his computer according to his computer he is safety in bed at ten o'clock. Benjamin thinks that time would be perfect to make an approach. Benjamin looked=s again this time he changes his mind he is thinking about half ten that's when he can make maximum carnage the more he thinks the better for him for some strange reason Benjamín watches the video, Benjamín does not know that the film that he is watching was way out of date and probably the wrong film. some body had been sending Benjamín the wrong information and he was just about to check the computer there may had been a fault. Benjamin figured it out almost straight away7, the police chef must have had some brilliant engineers as the information that was brought up onto Benjamín scene was all faze the man that Benjamín was watching was not the man that Benjamín was after he was a look alike quite common in the world of acting. Whoever made this film was extremely bad at it including thee editing.

Benjamin is getting anode as he looks for more information on the real target but there is not any, the police chief certainly knows how to cover his back. There was not a lot of information there anyway Benjamin tells his robot to keep on looking while he goes to look at the other information that his computer had gathered. Benjamin believes that it is a tip off all the information that he usually gets is the right information Benjamín believes that the target now does not even exist and if he does he is existing with a new name. Benjamín take one

more look repeatedly and again. Then out of the c=blue the computer finds him taking Benjamín back to the start.
COMPUTER:" He is in."
BENJAMIN:" what is the best time you can give, and I need a destination,"
COMPUTER:" he will be at home exactly ten past ten."
BENJAMIN: "can you pull address and give me a map."
COMPUTER:" yes give me a moment."
Benjamin finally releases the energy and the pressure disappears he has an address and within a few hours the target will be dead.

Oxygen and the hitman heard through the grape vine there was so much information on Benjamín the new bad guy on the seen you could have had a game of chinses whispers. It looked like the farmers had not given in and had told the police about what had happened during the experience of what occurred in the forest yesterday.

The police went straight to the scene, Benjamín crew were lucky, they had left no evidence the ship was built that well. They were looking for clues. However, the farmer was still in shock and his story was not making sense and the police only believed half of the story and the farmer that they were questioning needed a couple of pills to cram his down. The only evidence of t=what the man said was the half-broken gun left in the bushes. The gun went straight to forensics nothing came of it the cops were there for a day or two and could not find a thing even Benjamín tiger paws were covered the badge was quite clever. Oxygen stands there in the middle of the forest ground there was just enough space there was clearly some ground damage on the ground it was oblivious to them but not obvious to anybody else the oxygen could feel it was obvious that something had been there he thinks that the forest had been visited. The oxygen thinks that they have been visited he thinks that the ship was made to be light infect four large mud holes gave Benjamín away. there had defiantly been something have there. The oxygens question was what. The two cops discussed it more, hoping that they would find some more evidence. The oxygen had covered his tracks just in case the space being comes back. Benjamin had thought that he was safe as he also covered his tracks but his had been found. The oxygen and the hitman knew that the farmer was not lying and had experienced something above the normal. Benjamin was back on the earth.

The two cops baffled and did not know what to do.
OXYGEN:" I want aerospace, I'm going to Have to Make a call I want aerospace to come clean. There are handing something."
HITMAN:" I say tell them to make another move as we are on the ground."
OXYGEN:" that is a good idea, but it will just a matter pf time until we bump into him,"
HITMAN: "he's clever I have to give him that we must have just missed him the tracks that were left behind look reasonable fresh.
OXYGEN:" yeah we know he is up there and we down here, quite clever indeed."
HITMAN:" I want to know his next move."
OXYGEN:" I do not think that it matters."
HITMAN:" how can you say that"
OXYGEN:" I did not mean that last comment it is either that we are extremely bad at our jobs or e are being out classed by an alien.
HITMAN:" okay big boy wants the plan what is our next move I know that he is going to be in our city on planet earth am I right."

OXYGEN: "YES."
HITMAN: "There is a pattern to his killings the link is that they are of the city's most important and wealthy people. What you think that he is doing for the money."
OXYGEN:" No but he is doing it for something or someone. It makes me wonder who is next let's get out of here thus place is scaring me. Benjamin is still up above the clouds looking for information on the chiefs and his where about Benjamín is slowly running out of time. He calls on his robot for some help as he takes one more guess on where the target may be and with a click of a button they are on their way.
MARARTY:" Where is he."
MARARTY:" Benjamín he is at the hotel having a diner party."
BENJAMIIN: "well I have to say that's a fine way to go."
Mar arty smiles.
BENJAMIN: "Set the co-ordinations for the hotel."
His computer does so and then Benjamín finds out that the target can be seen by Benjamín and Benjamín believes he is being set up more and more imagines f=of the target are flooding in through the computer it was alike an art gallery art explosion. Benjamin computer has a lock on the target as the chief walks ion to his room greeting everybody Benjamín knew that he could just walk in, but he wants to wait. He is thinking that he has his target and waits to think of how he was going to do it. he moves towards his weapon cabinet.

He chooses a weapon and one bullet that was all it was going to take. As he was that good he is telling his computer and the robot to stay put not to make contact until they are told. Benjamin awaits in another building across the street e=well-hidden on the roof. It took Benjamín another few minutes to find the target and a just his riffle. As the chief the man that he was going to kill keeps on moving around and with other people around him but once he seated at his table his life was over and another one had just started. Benjamin had him in his sights he slips the bullet into the gun cartridge. And within a few second s had a scope on his target. Within another moment the chief of the police was dead, job done Benjamín calls apron his shipman the people in the room look around dazed and confused. The shot could not be heard as foe the make of the riffle. It had a silencer the only sound was the sound of the glass cracking as the bullet went into the

body. With the building being in a narrow street nothing the echoes of his people shouting in amazement could be heard.
As Benjamín calls for his Robot and asks him to make an approach to him as he is in the clear. The space ship was nearby, and Benjamin was picked up in a jiffy as be boards the ship he speaks to himself. As he gets a good look of what is left of the chief which was not a lot. Benjamin was pleased three down four to go.
Benjamin now must make an escape his turns up uncloaked, funny enough this time the escape was easy there was nobody around and all the people were down stairs in and on the streets. Although screaming and shouting could be heard. Benjamin boards his ship, he can feel the sorrow he has in side of him and around his soul. This was a knew feeling and thinks that he may have killed the wrong man. Benjamin is standing as he puts his phaser down. He looks at his computer and tells it the coordination's and tells him to take him there. Benjamin needs time to cool off there was nothing like above the clouds. Not forgetting that the man that he had just killed. He closes his eyes and falls to sleep.
The robot takes to the cockpit and gains control of the ship and the two sun flowers are talking amounts themselves both keeping an eye on things and keeping the robot company.
It was a few days until Benjamín had awoke the flowers had done their job. That was watching over him, and the planet earth. Benjami9n is still stuck in his space suit he continues that he was finding it hard to move around joking to the flowers who could see clearly that he was having a little trouble moving around.

Benjamin tells his robot to move over as Benjamín wants to take a seat. They were both sharing the chair. Looking down straight at the planet earth Benjamín starts a discussion about how long it was going to be there. With all the facts coming out, the robot compliments Benjamín as his knowledge was as good as his. His knowledge was in fact perfect. They continued to discuss it through out of the day until his robot asked him to stop. As the robot said this is over load started meaning that he needed to charge himself up after a few sparks Benjamin knew that he was serious and not bowing out of the conversation because he had been beaten for knowledge.

Benjamin laughs the robot tells him that it is no joke. The planet earth was serious business it was there business now.

Benjamin replies to the robots last words are the humans really that bad. Are they really destined for their own destruction?

The robot answers with you said destruction. They start a new conversation and had started talking about the wars of the planets past. They were both hitting each other with perfect reply's and beating each other disagreements with correct answers. It had become a verbal argument from a serious but friendly conversation. Benjamin new what had happened the robot was just expressing itself and its compo ants as Benjamín did his mind. They both finally conclude that the planet was doomed because the humans did not care for it enough.

CHAPTER NINE
IN DEEP WATER

Benjamin was board of being in OutSpace or there about even more so being up in the earth's ozone. He wants to go back down to the earth he was thinking under the sea the ocean. He already knew that there was a possible chance of the ship being found by the submarines, but he was going to take a chance he tells the robot that heat might be fun being chased again by a couple of submarines. He taps in the coordinates and makes a quick departure from space to the ocean water. His space ship was also built to move underwater, he finds somewhere to rest his ship it was a nice sand bank at the bottom of the ocean. He had taken the ship right down to the bottom of the sea. Benjamin begins to settle as he is watching the wild life and is finally relaxed. It ws one of his favourite places on the earth or should I say under it.

Benjamin enjoys the views he seems to be with one with himself and everything that surrounds him. The robot wants to join in and is getting excited and the flowers Aare chanting it seemed to Benjamín that it was a good idea after all as everybody was happy. As they all watch the sea life.as the time went by the smaller fish in the sea were departing and the larger sea life were coming out to play.

Within a few minutes Benjamín ship is surrounded by sharks they know that Benjamin is there, and they were swimming closer and closer Benjamín is fascinated and closes his eyes. Some of the shark's bump on the ship Benjamín believes that it is a warning just to let Benjamín know that they are there. Benjamin is cool about it as he leans over to a small fridge he opens it and pulls a can of beer out of the fridge door side still half watching the sharks.

As he puts his feet up on top of his dashboard he opens the can of v=beer. The sharks were now getting more and more violet they defiantly knew that there were some kinds of presents there. Benjamin still was just happy to sit there.

Although the robot was not to keen and looked as little bit worried. As much as the robot liked the sea life in the day time in the night time it made him feel uneasy under the water he was all over the place and would not stop saying more oxygen I cannot breathe and on top of that sharks.

Benjamin although humoured takes control of the situation and turns his robot off, it was nice and quiet again. As the sea life slowly depart Benjamín is left with the full view of the sandy floor. And the full view of the ocean above.

Benjamin had not ever had the chance to experience being under the ocean before or had not had the opponent to swim in the sea. He had begun dreaming maybe that's why he was drawn to this place under the ocean waters.

As Benjamín sits and continues to watch there are all kinds of life emerging around him as he watches from the inside of his ship. He had not yet learnt the names of the species that are entertaining him. He wanted to know all the names of these new creatures he watches in extrapolation. And falls fond of it. it was even more angering as he was falling in love with being amount them. he wanted to know if they could communicate with them. As he has puzzled himself with his own thought over them.

Benjamin closes his eyes and falls asleep with the new thought he dreams of being on his home planet the robot wants to surface he ws scared of that type of wild life Benjamín tells it to put the thought in to his mind as the robot was just about to decide Benjamín give s in and tell the robot to take the ship up and back up above the earth. The robot takes the ship up of the ocean floor and surfaces junta foot above the ocean waves. The robot feels a lot better Benjamín was in a sulk as he was enjoying himself. Benjamin knows that there is going to be trouble Benjamín and his crew stay put.

In the meantime, Oxygen and the hitman a few days later turn up at Benjamín last items scene any gain they find nothing it was the same except before they time to get there the police had cleared the scene. Everything had to go conferences and ballistics they needed to know what kind of bullet it was when they got there the bullet shell matched the one that came out of the body of the item and fitted the now empty cartage although there is no match for the bullet it defiantly did not come from the earth. Oxygen and the hitman were surprised, they knew that they were on the right tracks. They were both thinking the same.
OXYGEN: "It sure looks like our little play mate has a thrust for blood."

It was obvious that the bullet was from an alien weaned and the Oxygen and the Hitman discuss every detail. They were still on the roof where the shot was taken. They were talking about how much security that the target had and weather it ws adequate. The Oxygen believing that he was poorly guarded either that or the man who shot was an extreme special shot. The hitman continues he believe s that it was the same man and now they were looking for a serial killer. Oxygen agrees and could see where the conversation was going. Oxygen could not make himself any clearer, looking at the evidence.

CHAPTER TEN
CODE

Benjamin needed a code to get inside their systems, but the code was not with me or in my mind I had not got the message that I was being followed by an Assassin and I was an assassin. There was going to be lightning and thunder I could feel the wither changing in my sleep. as I laid in my capsule fast asleep I was dreaming of my next target it was to be a shop assistant. I had taken in consideration that this target was going to be easy. I had not taking inconsideration of this target as he was a young man and going to be a dead one by the computer. I closed my eyes and fell back asleep looking for more information on him hoping that the dream would bring it and tell me the rest. I was in my chair and not in my bunk not that it made any difference. The images of the things that this young man had done were piling up I could see everything clearly. It ws like watching a film of myself everything that I had ever done everything that I had ever seen. Since that I had approached the planet earth. I was just waking up with the knowledge that I had received in my sleep. I cannot explain it right now, but it was extremely interesting. As I woke up in a cold sweat. I was drenched I did not know whether it came from my mouth or my mind as I awoke I floated through the space ship thinking about the next kill. Meantime the two cops down on the earth were thinking of my last kill I believe that there was no evidence as I had cleaned it all away they could never blame me as the bullet that I used came from my planet and did not exist on the earth.

They thought that they were clever, but I was trice as educated as them. I floated around towards my computer. The robot had recorded everything, this is where it hurt the memories, the remorse, and the thought of killing them. I now knew that I had missed the target somehow, I, are the mistake as I took his soul into my body I had realised that I had killed the wrong man.

I was chilled even though I had missed the target and I was still cool even though I could feel some anger for stupidity I knew that I was good enough to make another attempt.

I wanted to go back to the woods, but I feared that I would raise suspicion all over again and I knew that it would be trouble.

There was a bounty on my head this time it was a real one. I guess that I could always go back to the bottom of the sea. It might be safer down there than up here, a part of the submarines. I could decide given a bit of time as, so I decided to stay amongst the clouds or just above them. The flowers were teasing me over what had happened the robot did not make a sound even though he wanted to say something I could tell by the look on his face. I told them all to shut up even though none of them were speaking.

I had to make a report, so I just got on with it. I was beginning to think that thing s were going to go wrong and that scared me.

Even though I had faith some people might think I was short of it. At that point I closed my eyes it was all I could do. I fell asleep knowing that I would find the answer and peace.

The dream that in was having of the third victim to me seemed pointless it was of the normal boy a human Benjamín can see no wrong in him and had only a few hours before had all the information on his entire life little it may be short. It was insignificant to the plan. Benjamin tells his computer that he is confused. It was now too late to go back home to get the real facts it was just to late. Benjamin closed his eyes this time leaving his mind his semi consciousness it was rally that he would do that in his sleep, but he did not that he could sleep in fact he had not slept at no point when he was on the earth. It seemed to him that the planet was really doomed he wanted to know something that was where the plans that his planet were having were they about saving the planets future., either way I reminded myself that humans had sold itself out. And it was my job to make sure that the deal is done.

Benjamin was on the planet following the boy along. His movements were as usual pretty much the same. I had been following him for a couple of weeks it still did not make any sense. The next hit was rattling Benjamín s brains he turns to the computer and got nothing he turned to his robot who finds the solution. That the boy was put there to confuse the situation Benjamín quickly understood and was happy that he had an excuse, so he did not have to take the young boys life. Benjamin knows now that he is being set up. Benjamin takes to the cockpit and takes his ship up in to space into a place that he felt safe. He was nice and relaxed and waiting he was still thinking about the boy he ws thinking that he would let him go. He knows that it was a mistake to take the council and make decisions on them behave but on this occasion, he did just that, he was beginning to think that he was losing his mind. Any other time he would have just done the job in hand. In the end Benjamin bows down to his council he could feel the power of all of them thinking for him he knows that he must kill the boy target he loads up his phaser steps out of the space craft he knows all the boys moves and waits until he in front of him. He wanted the boy to him as boy just stands innocently Benjamín raises his arm the boys raise his arms and then speaks asking him if he was under rest no Benjamín continues your dead. But something was wrong it was not in my nature to kill the innocent I'm sure that somewhere down the line there was a mistake the boy knew I could not do it and I knew that I could not do it vi had been sent the wrong target again.

Benjamin believes now that he was being set up to fail and was on his way back to his home planet what impressed him the most that the boy was willing to take the bullet. Once I was back on the space ship plugged in the coordinates and buckled everybody in, I was doing this fast as that is the way I moved.

Benjamin wanted to speak to his council about his next kill the next victim I could see that they had done know wrong. the kind of thought that Benjamín was having were of trees and murder the council was there straight away and as they all appeared I started to put my complaint forwards.

After a long meeting they finally agreed that they might have wrongly entered his systems believing that his was somebody else they also agreed that the killing were just, and they said that I let the boy go. Benjamin was pleased not knowing approaching the council was a mistake as in the future the council's truth would come out it ws a big mistake by him and a bigger mistake by the commanders however Benjamín had convinced them for now.

The councillors last words were before the meeting ended were we have given the boy a chance, but it means nothing.

I put aside as I had better business to do it was not nearby as I could have been doing other things. I went for the next target not forgetting the chief of the police which I also got a grilling for by the council. The next target was a prisoner I had to get this one right or that would be the end for me as it was also just spoken about in the council rooms. I could not afford to make any more mistakes. This guy the prisoner he was basically running the city's underworld from his prison cell. Everything that moved in and everything that moved out this guy was a real scum bag he was a daddy the big daddy. I changed the coordinates and moved the space ship. It was time to use the suit again as checked if the suit was fully charged and keeping one eye on the time I had all his details running through my mind everything my escape then NY approach and how many guard s were there and even what his reaction would be before I got there.

I was getting closer I could feel his sickness I was nervous that was the first time that I felt worried it was not like me. in could make the hit that is all my mins =d would let me say. As I morphed myself in to invisibility it seemed like I could just walk in, but it was walking out which was going to be the problem. It was in their ground s that I had found the game had begun it did not take belong to find him, but he had so many covers it was hard to get to him. I had failed again my superior were not happy they could see that I could see that.

Benjamin had told his guardians his saviours that he could not make the hit there were to many doors and people about he reacted fiercely to what Benjamín had said they were unhappy and were discussing whether Benjamín could do his job. Even more so weather or not he was good end ought to do his job. I was being pulled aside as Benjamín had lost his temper. There were many answers to why Benjamín did not full fil his missions. They were many questions which were going unanswered as Benjamín did not know the answers to the questions that were being thrown at him. He loses his temper again. In the end the council gave Benjamín a bit of le way. They gave him the chance to do his job again their words were do not fail us. Benjamin told them that he needs time to think, they agree. He leaves the court room and goes to his room when he gets there the robot is there to greet him Benjamín is tired and pushes the robots welcoming, Benjamin lie down on his bed. Then greets the robot. He was happy that the boy had be granted amnesty it makes it better for Benjamin one less person to kill. As he dreams he see everything knowing that he must go way back into the past to see where he went wrong and if he can catch up with the two corrupt targets as he dreams he hears the word s you have been sucking up and he was a squalor a big mouth. With no control verbally or mentally. He woke up in the end while dreaming of putting a bullet in some guys head it was a nightmare. In the dream it retook Benjamin a day and a =n evening to find him as I awoke I was still on the planet but in my room. Benjamin grabbed mar arty and headed to my space craft the bullet that he was dreaming about was for him he was making a quick escape.

I made my way back to the space ship something was not right it seemed to me that I had a hit on a target which had a hit on me which I should not have hit. I knew that I was going to have nightmares over this one. However, if name was on the list then his name his on the list. As the boy did not fit in I think that I found the real target I left the body on the road where it could be found. Within a few hours the cops both were on the scene. Oxygen is taking a close look while the hitman locks around thinking if this was Benjamin. As Benjamin thinks that he ships was cloaked the two cops get a glimpse of something that they think is not there Benjamin is watching clearly and realizes that his cloak is off as he switches it on the two cops draw their weapons.
OXYGEN: "Did you see that."
THE HITMAN: "yeah I did."
OXYGEN:"
Oxygen and Hitman raise their arms believing that they had found the target Benjamin meanwhile as they approach the ship is turning everything off telling the computer to shut everything down as he recloaks his ship and takes it ten feet up into the air. They did not fully approach Benjamin, but they knew that his presents were there I believed that they saw the shape of the ship and that's all.

After the close encounter he decided that I should go home back to my planet and council at that time I did not know that I could only approach the planet if I was invited. As I walked in to the great halls un invited the councillors began to question right there I was trying to tell them about the experience back on the planet earth.

The council began to question me first telling me that I was wrong to approach them at this time the conversation went on for hours all over the target that I had missed I began to complain, telling again over and over that the computer was in control at that time and it was not his mistake but their s and the computers. I had just enough evidenced to convince them that I was only trying to do my job. The sentence for this was doing time this time I had lost. I thought that this was a little harsh I knew the planet that they would be sending me too. The conversation went on and on the council, were being extremely hard it was still unknown to them that the silhouette was still breathing down my neck. Up to the point that I stared a fight with him as I pushed him to the floor then telling him to get up. As he I floored him again it took everything in my powers to try and convince them that my words were true, and I was stalling the truth. At this point the council decided to re-evaluate and kindly asked me to start again a new interview. This was going to be the hardest thing of my life and the evidence was against me. I as wit coming the silhouette was just getting off the floor as he raised his sword as he was now behind me and was about to attack me, as the council laid witness to it the guards that were supposed to protect me did not they just stood there. The first time he missed yelling that he had had enough the second end time I was on the floor with his sword against my chest he moved backward s removing the sowed from me. and started all again I was looking for my sword, but I did not have one according to the councillor know weapons are allowed in the court room I was lucky as they could clearly see that it was not me that was braking their laws. I could feel it he ws hoping that I would use the badge he was trying to set me up. I wanted to show the council that it was me that was full of goodness but, yet I was still the betrayer. The silhouette drops his sword realizing where he was and kneels on the floor even though with a bad temper he ws still calm. I knew that I could not continue with his personal battle as I was unarmed. As he had got up on his feet and was now slowly moving around me in a circle he talking to me it like he was putting curse upon me. I could feel every word as he walked behind me again this time calling me a liar he raises his sword for the third time as he was about to stake me down. The guards move in, the guards grab hold of him but not begore he strikes one down, He falls to his knees still talking to the council his words were let me kill him as the silhouette shouts he is dragged out of the great hall. After the events in the court room Benjamin is given amnesty and he was free to go. But not before he bows down to the silhouette as I walked towards him knowing now dangerous he was Benjamin greeted him polity and bowed my head.

Benjamin ws hesitant but happy that he can now go on his way. When I had got home I tapped my security code into the door lock, but it did not open, I tried again I was confused. As I tried again then again, I got the same answer as I turned around I bumped straight in to some guards three of them in fact I was thinking at that time that I was at the wrong address. The had me in a corner they were not being particularly nice as they shave dame around a little, the fist guard tapped me on the back I had turned my back to them to give me time to think. It did not work, I was s being set up again as the guard continued to prod me I knew not to turn around but to answer them. and that is all I can remember about that encounter as hard as I was theatre was no way that I could beat them without the space to change. When I awoke I was on a totally different planet I had been kidnapped I awoke in chains in a cell the bed was broken, and its pillow was on the other side of the room. There was a basin and a toilet on the side of the cell in its corner. I wanted to call out, but I could not speak it felt like I was on something I had been poisoned. At that point I was thinking that I was losing the gift to communicate. I could feel my eyes it looked like I took a bit of a beating on top of things. As I tried to call out there was nothing I was trying to think where I was if I could find my new destination I could send a message to my robot and computer to hail them. As I waited for my voice to return I could clearly see that there was a jug of water on the side, I ws beaten I just wanted to kick something it would have been better if my hand sewer untied I would be able to pick it up.

As I sat down with no food or heat every day for the next few years was a nightmare in the end I was now beginning to break no food nothing a cup of water at the very least. I was smashing rocks day in and day out still did not speak to anybody even that my voice had grown back. I was into keeping myself to myself. And when was approached I told the person to leave me I ws not in the business of making friend I was an assassin. I was breaking rocks and the food everyday was getting worse and worse not that I would eat any of it as I was supplied with everything through my suit.

The food was basically a hand full of vegetables and a cup of water I called it my brothers laugh sane was giving my portion to the guy that I was chained to but only when I was working on the grounds. As many times that he had thanked me I still did not speak to him.

The cells were cold and with no light and the darkness was the only place that I wanted to dwell.

After the beating s and the whippings, I was beginning to give in I ws looking at the stars calculating the exact time by the stars it was coming up to my fourth year of prison. My space ship still had not turned up. Every so often the guards would come in to the cell and try and remove the suit from me. I cannot count how many time s they had tried it was just a matter of time before my robot would find a way of finding me I was pledging all my confidents in him.

It was no use at this moment a few past I was truly screwed I could hear my consciousness telling me everything that was going to happen to me I was still in touch but only just meanwhile back on in the councillor's room they believed that I had one a runner and was handing on the planet earth they sent their assassins the silhouette too finds me when he told them he could find me he was punished also.

A cargo ship came by every two weeks leaving more prisoners and it ws heavily guarded the shackles that I was wearing did not leave me room to maunder as for the guy that was chained to did not make the planed escape any easier. Every time the ship came I just bowed and the thought of sorrow that I was left there on the concrete. I must have dug a thousand metres in the planets soil. The thought of it was not helping it was become at that point adductive in the end I felt I could not work on longer I weak and tried and starved there was nothing left of me. I had fallen on to my knees, I had become a slave that was far from being the super human that I was before I was brought here. The suit was not working either the prison girds had smashed it so hard with me in. as I was just about to give up I could see something approaching the court yard they looked like the guards back in the councillors Greta halls as the ship lined the guard s walked out. The guards were ordering everybody to lie down as I was about to lay on the floor one of the guards stooped me and he spoke his words where you are free come with us. I raised up my shackles he pointed his weaned down on the ground ignoring the man that I was attached to and within a second my feet were freed. the pensicner swore cheering as he realises the shackles around Benjamin's wrists. They march him away. Benjamin could not believe it he was free and extremely happy.my space ship had landed I felt sorry for some of those people aa lot of them were innocent, I viewed to that day that I would come back with justice.

After I had been taken back to my quarters after the councillors had interviewed me I was taken away to be cleaned up after I had renewed my suit and was greeted by the robot and the sunflower s I was asked to stay around until I was fully nourished in my new suit after a while may be a few days my normal way of thinking came back, and I was thinking about who set me up. I was on my way back to the planet earth to finish the job.

My robot brought me my new suit I was happy to take it as I was shaving the long grey beard off I ws talking to the robot. I ws telling him that I had not ever felt that weak. Anand as weak as I was I cleaned my sleeve up again. As I walked out of the bath room I could see that the robot had brought my two sun flowers to great me and they were happy and as entertaining as always.
I changed my clothes and was back in the suit again. The robot did not want to tell me as he thought that it would hurt Benjamin, but he could not lie and told Benjamin that it was the silhouette that had set him up. Benjamin told the robot that he knew that already. And told him not to mention his right now we will talk bout it another time and I will approach the council when I am called. The robot agrees. As Benjamin had closed his eyes he was sending his mind not in one the future but back to it, he sees that there had been a great argument and the silhouette had destroyed the council and made another one by his name. as Benjamin wore the suit he had the right to approach him but only if invited he could see that happening soon. Benjamin wants to get out of the planet quickly, Benjamin was going to depart back to the earth but first he takes a glimpse of his future.

The robot went off on one as Benjamin and its self were boarding the space ship Benjamin jumps in the cockpit as he is setting the ship up for take-off the robot is still talking about the planet and they are having the conversation as Benjamin taps the coordinates the planet earth. He knows already that he was going to be followed that was the last of Benjamin worry's as he must save his own planet at the same time.
A new council had been made Benjamin could understand why. A new council was about them and they were brought more peace as Benjamin raises his ship up to take off. he could feel that the people were not happy as much as Benjamin wanted to stay around he had a

job on the planet earth. Benjamin new that there was going to be rioting. It was out of his hands at this moment. As much as he wanted too to stay he was explaining to the robot he had to leave this played on Benjamin's consciousness for a while as he taps in the coordinates to the earth. The robot had so many questions that it would twist your mind. He continued they said that they wanted peace, yet they were killing their innocent their very own peace keepers for speaking of peace.

I ws thinking that the planet ws not governed enough and soon it will destroyed and there was nothing that we would be able to do but turn to the planet earth. It was not in our nature, but I had to close n=my eyes again asking myself questions after questions why was I thinking the worst.
It was not my job to do the thinking, it was my job to kill. I closed my eyes yet again for another time I was counting on the thought to leave. If the council knew what I was thinking they would have me in the council room again a d judged.

As I made my way back into space as I approached the earths solar system I was heading straight for the planet it was night time as I waited for the night time after the second morning I was back in the wood s testing out the new suit this time it came with head gear I was hoping that I would not disturb any thing I did not want the farmers coming after me again. I already knew the powers of the suit I could morph in to a tiger I could also have invisibility and I could weld a shield. I ws now thinking and getting g more excited I was going to tap the badge for a fourth time to see what would happen as I did after wasting all the energy on the frill of the badge there ws nothing I was impressed but confused I restate badge with my mind and tried again and again nothing. I was doing something wrong. I called the robot outside.

With my robot by my side I did it again the same thing happened again for some strange reason the robot was refused to help me he said that on this one Benjamin had to figure it out for himself. After an hour I had to give up it was getting dark Benjamin steps absurd the ship and cloaks it. temerity is waiting. And asks Benjamin if he had any luck on that point the robot and Benjamin sit down and discuss the history of the badge where it came from who knows its true power and everything else and especially how it was found, there was an extremely long story to the badge and its makers.

According to the story the third part of the badge needs to hear the wearers voice and the word is that are to be spoken are the word and number S P I R I T 5. Benjamin is excited as now that he has the robots word he can continue with the study of the badge. Except it is dark the right place to tune and re energise his suit but the wrong time to play with it.

Benjamin was willing to give it another go but he would have to wait until sun rise believing in badge and its words.

Again, nothing had happened the robot tells him to say it with politely and say it like you mean it as I did the third power was their like it came out of nowhere, but Benjamin still could not figure it out. h knew what the robot was going to say figure it out for yourself. Benjamin was frustrated knowing that the robot had the answer and would not tell him.

Benjamin is delighted by the power od=f the badge even though he cannot find the fourth power he as the morning come he is outside trying to figure it out and not having much luck. He starts with under tapping the badge and keeps commanding its shelled the idea qasr simple enough, Benjamin just needed a bit more time. As he sits there weighing up the odds that that within a couple of days tab police will back. In the meantime, he would stay put in the forest and try and figure out the next super power of the suit. Benjamin just thought that he should look around the forest as it seemed to him to be a nice and quiet place and the wither was holding as he walks he keeps on getting the urge to run in the end he gives in and breaks out in to a sprit he had found the fourth power of the badge stealth. As he moves faster and faster unseen he was feeling good as he makes it back to his space ship he is happy to tell the robot who in return congratulates him. Benjamin is happy.

Benjamin sits down in his bunk he is tried as much as the day, the gift that he received that morning made him feel. As the night comes quickly he thinks of the next and last super power as he has now super speed stealth. He was feeling excellent and wants to practice more he was becoming more and more confident. Benjamin wants to go outside the robot warns not to over indulged and now is worried Benjamin ignore s the robot's advice and heads outside any way a little unusual fir Benjamin the robot tells him to be careful Benjamin reptile what's the worst that could happen. As Benjamin practices the skills of the badge through the night he getting better and better as he get used to it and good at it he spend sell day clicking g and unclicking his badge until he tired he walks back to his space ship completely exhausted all he wants to do is lie down he is tried again before he gets the chance to settle down the robot is there talking to him telling him that the bounty hunters and the famer were back, became knows why he has left his ship uncloaked as he thought it would be safe handing in the darkness of the forest.

There are no weapons on the ship as it is a ship of peace Benjamin stand sin full view if the bounty hunters he is feeling tired and die snot know if he has the energy to full fill the battle which was ahead. The crowed of people are shouting at him he is feeling more and more for the fight as Benjamin is being told not to harm any of them and must think of a way of other's approaching them or getting back into his space ship and fin ding another destination. Benjamin could see clearly that he was going to be in the morning papers again.

FARMER:" I told you, I told you that he ws their but none of you believed it."

Benjamin was going to try Ans reason with them now that's all he could do.

The robot just tells him to make something up. Benjamin's reply to that was what I am standing here in front of a mob.

The robot tells Benjamin to tell them that he is an experiment from American aerospace.

Benjamin does not think that it would work but he tried it. with a little bit of work to the that last comment things were looking a little bit quieter the robot was telling him to play along Benjamin had never had the chance to act he was getting into the role quickly.

As more and more questions were put to him he finally told the that he was smeary here to protect the environment and that it. he continues that the space was all part of the programme to scare the Germans.

They finally agree, and they leave Benjamin alone again. Benjamin walked d back on to his ship bursting into laughter that was hilarious your clever little robot I have never had so much fun. The crowed disperse and the farmer gets it in the neck again.

BENJAMIN: "You could have given them a chance at least one."

MARATRTY: "It is my job to protect you. Tat what I did now get on the space ship please."

Benjamin does as he is told and gets on the space ship. He continues the conversation the returns answers for his actions the robot even though Benjamin had not opened fire and killed the group of men he knew that it was protocol and he was now getting a grilling like what it would come out when he gets his summoning to the council.

After the long conversation with the robot as tired as Benjamin was they both shut themselves down the robot plugs its self in for a re-charge and Benjamin lays out on his bed, the sun flowers are singing him to sleep. this time there's no dreams just crying as Benjamin's upset over the last days out goings as he trees to tune ate radio and in the end, get fed up throwing it across the room only for gravity to put it back into his hands. As he plays around with it as he pushes it away leaves it floating around the ship. Benjamin finally settles down Benjamin is worried, as he must dream of the silhouette he knows that he is close to him but only in his mind. The silhouette was not the man you would want in your mind the thought of thinking of him could destroy you. Either way I was going to put up a fight.

CHAPTER ELEVEN
BROKEN CIRCUTS

Ass I thought about who set me up and gave me a good five years I ws concluding that it was the silhouette the though sent ne back five years thinking that I as lucky, but the pain still existed. Every thought every fear of what could have happened and what happened. Back then I knew that it ws name it was not knowing s to me I could see clearly, I just wanted my revenge. I thought about him more and more as until I believed that I was now in his mind rather than him being in mine. I was trying to thin k about other things the d=good thing and the dad things it was not easy, but I was getting it right for now. I did not think that the silhouette knew that I knew, and we were both playing the game the thoughts of him were taking me to the edge and likewise I was driving him crazy. He wanted my badge, I could not give it to him you see it was awarded to me and once the badge was on it could not be removed, valour by the council unless he was up there making new rule is the badge stays on. He had none, I knew that if we were e to come to battle I would win. He did not k now that I was playing the same game as him from now. I put myself into his mind this time with the badge as my guidance, as my weaponeer, I might have a chance to destroy him and that was all to come.

Thinking about him was given me a trill. Thinking what was going to happen in the future ws giving Benjamin a cold sweat and enough thought's. Benjamin tyres to think and he goes over it like a script repeatedly until he finds the answer and is happy again. It was finally sinking in, but it would eventually pass. As I had business son the planet earth. Her was salt to think about the destruction of my home planet had happened that was what the robot was trying to tell me it happened while I was in orison and the destruction of our seven guests which was opt he earths planets hope.

If the silhouette gains power, he will destroy everything I was not going to let that happen. I was concerned for the planet who would not be. as I spoke to the robot letting him know that I knew that my family were dead through the court by the silhouette and his destructive behaviour.

I had enough of sorrow and I was on my way back to earth I knew who the target was it ws the boy gain again I was trying to resist and I knew this time that the council controlling=g the killing was not to be messed around with I had no choice be=vein though I has=d feeling =s to the job. I did not have time to gain the ken obliged to make it look sweet I just had to kill him as he left his shop as us I was there it was straight forward I pulled my gun and took a good look at him within the next couple second she was dead two bullets threw the chest, he knew and I knew it was his time after I had killed him I looked at the body but only for a minute as I walked away it was time to give the police a call. I was thinking how I was going to use the suit.

Something had gone wrong I was projected in to the future and I was at the next hit the next target I knew where ea. was but I did not know why it had happened after the hit of the boy the power of the thought had sent me way into y=the future I did not have to do thing I was right infant of my target as I sat in the middle of the room because e in a corner would be to obovoid I hid behind a paper the ___ 14 old fashioned d way to spy I saw the target but before I had a chance to eliminate him form the list something strange happened again I was back looking at the body of the boy. when I got back to my ship to explain to the robot what I had just experienced thaw robot could not find answer as he was not present it looked like Benjamin had to figure it out for himself.

As I walked back to the space ship I was feeling anger over what I had just killed even though the thought in the café was a calming one the force of killing somebody so young ws hurting me. my space ship had arrived, and I walked on up into the cargo bay and on to the ship.

BENJAMIN:" What's going on."

ROBOT:" It Seems to me that there is pattern to are killing this has to be= changed."

BENJAMIN:" it does not make a difference the outcome Is the same."

ROBOT: "I know it is just harder. I do not know the answer all I know is that the chief was supposed to be next."

BENJAMIN:" That does not make it any easier.

As the whole thing went through my mind feeling like my old self again. As I went to find some where to calm down I found a café it was extremely busy, and I looked out of place through this I could not get served at the counter I place d myself down at one of the tables a few minutes later as a waiter came to me I asked for as black coffee and she took the order within a few more minute I was feeling better. I was looking at the menu I walked out forgetting the order and left the café the waiter was not too far behind me and I told her to forget it as I had to be somewhere. She looked up set and I was just as confused, As for the expression on the face.
BENJAMIN:" It cannot make any=difference a hit is a hit am I right I cannot go home because it is no longer there. What is the answer, answer me?"
Benjamin for the first time loses his r=temper, the robot is confused to see hemin that state Benjamin tells the computer to turn all the systems off and asks his robot to help him to his bunk he knew exactly what it was the new suit was setting in. knowing that now he must find and climate with no excuses the targets as he thinks of this in his sleep he also knows that he is in danger. He knows that he was to blame and if he did blame somebody it would be the computer even more so himself. He tells the computer to take him back into the past he has the victims address he taps in the coordinates and makes his way there while Benjamin talks to his computer it explains why he ws miss guided and why he got the target wrong the first time. This time it was the chief. Benjamin steps outside of the dark shadows of the street the road swore half lit as he watches the chief from up=underneath a large tree. The chief is making his way up his garden path Benjamin believes that it was the right time to make the kill. As the chief unlocks the door Benjamin a=can to catch up with him as the chief unlocks the door he walks in side closing the door as Benjamin just gets there it ws right tp0 the point of being in his face. the chief turns on the living room lights and pours himself a drink.

The cop knows that he has got company and makes it easy for Benjamin to film=ND him. The chief is no coward he was a killer and he was fed up with the game he was fed up with his life. Benjamin walks in techier has his back to him. As he puts down the tumbler glass on to the table which was near to him. He continues to talk to Benjamin, Benjamin could see exactly what he ws doing he was trying to talk himself out of it. Benjamin tells him that he is no god and if he was looking for him he would better look hard. Benjamin tells him that he is there to kill him. Benjamin does not mess around the chief turns around again showing him Benjamin's back as turns around again Benjamin gets a good look at him, making sure this time it was the right person the right target. It was not a fake dressed up in a police uniform. Benjamin takes a step forwards and raises his arm. A few minutes later Benjamin walks out of the house the chief was dead. As he walks down the drive way he calls for his robot and space ship to find him and pick him up. Eventually the ship turns up, as the police do Benjamin can see the ship even though it is cloaked the hanger bay doors open and Benjamin steps aboard.
BENJAMIN:" Robot you are cutting it fine where have you been."
ROBOT:" Err yes well' I could not find you, bad weather. |"
As Benjamin talks to his computer tell it to record the and wants a picture of the dead target the chief, a close of the body. Once it had been taken out of the house. There are more and more cars coming and the colonel had turned up also. This make Benjamin believe that there on to him again Benjamin must make a session and quick.

Benjamin knows that they know that he can be invisible as for the last time they met.

OXYGEN:" I want you to search the whole area I believe that he is still in the area."

The hitman walks in to the house he could visualized every that had happened he could even see the image of the body before and after it was deceased. It looked like it was a hit to him. After he come s out if the house he walks to the body for one last look. He tells the forensic team to take the body away.

OXYGEN: "Is he dead."

HITMAN: "Yes, two bullets to his chest, killed him instantly."

OXYGEN: "I guess that there no pay rise for us this year."

Hitman: "knock it off this is not a joke.

The two cops finish at the scene and call it off they get back into the car the cool one drives off. The rest of the police so disperse.

As the last police car disappears down the road its silent again, for some strange reason Benjamin decides to stay around on the ground and zoom in to space. After he had taken a good look at everything he come back and get back on to his ship. As he sits down in the cockpit seat he starts dreaming of being under the sea. As Benjamin falls asleep the robot takes control he gives s Benjamin a surprise as he takes the ship back to earth and in to the ocean. The robot plugs the coordinates and within a minute they are off. The robot is getting good he then turns the computer on it ws voice activated and tells it to play some music, classical of course, for the journey. As Benjamin is sleeping they zoom off into the night and eventually finding the earths coast line as they make their way across the ocean and down underneath it to the cold ocean floor as the robot settles the ship Benjamin wakes up in his favourite place. He was not particular happy but thank full.

He sits up in his seat and watches the life underneath the sea.

As Benjamin is under the sea he sees what is happening to the ocean as he watches what was a left of the wild life. It ws so peace full. Benjamin thanks the robot for taking him there. Benjamin is taking to the Ron=bot and computer about what it would be like to dive and opens a discussion with the booth of them one that he thought would win but he does not. Benjamin is telling the robot that he wants to explore the ocean the robot does not think much on Benjamin s request. The robot tells Benjamin it could probably take a few years it was a vast place. Benjamin finally gives in and tells the robot the it was a silly thought and he was right they had no time Benjamin is disappointed.

As he slumps back into his chair and continues to watch the sea life around him the robot goes off for a re-charge.

CHAPTER TWELVE
TIME TO PARTY

Benjamin is desperate to know what it would like to swim under the ocean. He is drawn by it beauty and its power Benjamin so despite top know what it would be like to swim under the ocean. He is drawn in by its beauty and its power he could see it and dream about it all day long.
Erich what he was doing. He calls to his computer he is casemated and tells it to find some pitchers Benjamin was busy trying to find what the

humans called deep sea diving. Benjamin see=tidy's what we call deep sea divers. Benjamin watches and study the information that the commuter brings to him. Intensively and delighted after wards he goes to his cargo bay looking for some oxygen tanks which he had just seen on serein via his computer, he does not have any. He is disappointed there ws only one way od's =f doing this and that was going back up to the earths surface and finding land.
Benjamin was excited about what he was he might be doing in the future. he searches for another things way=his robot. Eventually he finds s a surf shop which would sell diving equipment. As he speaks to hides robot.
BENJAMIN: "Is this stuff good."
ROBOT: "Yeah it is safe just do not take the mouth piece out of your mouth. Or you will drown."
BENJAMIN: "Drown."
ROBOT: "Yes drown, you will suffocate."
BENJAMIN:" Explain again
ROBOT: "There is nothing to it once you have your suit on you just put the tank which is full of oxygen that's is h2o on your back over your suit. Then all you will do is jump into the water but remember that you can only breathe through the mouth piece without it you will suffocate and probably drown."
BENJAMIN:" That does not sound very nice."
ROBOT: "If you drown that will be the end of you, so be careful."
Benjamin is still a little confused but thinks he understands the ins and the outs of it. Benjamin leans back in his chair with the look of delight in his face. he was getting e3xcited, the sun flowers had started to laugh, and morality seems the same he was happy too.
Although there were still a few things on Benjamin's mind like the next job and the cops that were following him around knowing that the cops knew that all the murders were all linked and were pray=try close on catching him how ever Benjamin already knew this. Benjamin wants the facts as he -sends his mind back into the past he treys to re-call the insolent on the roof on top of the building and when he was stuck in between them one of them mentioned a name.

Benjamin thinks and thinks until he is confused in his mind and finds the answer that he ws looking for now knowing that the cops were trailing him. Benjamin closes his eyes and within a few minutes find s

him that was easy Benjamin says his name to himself. Oxygen. That was what he was called Benjamin has found one of the cops.
Benjamin ws now thinking that he can use the name of the cop to hack into the city. Of course, blaming the cop. As Benjamin also now knows that he is being followed beaming wants to know how close to them he was and was thinking weather or not he was in the position of being caught.
COMPUTER:" There is an eighty percent chance that you will get caught."
BENJAMIN; "Even if we are under the water."
COMPUTER:" Yes unfortunately."
Benjamin sighs.
BENJAMIN:" Computer give me everything that you have on the oxygen."
The computer bilges the cop has two names and his address with some other personal stuff comes up onto the screen his cars number plate stating that they both drive fast. Benjamin believes that the information came up on to the computer t=way too quickly they wanted to be found or that they were extremely stupid.

Benjamin has a massive profile on his screen in front of him of the copper they call oxygen on the planet earth. Benjamin has everything from his shoes size to the colour of his underpants, to the colour of his eyes. Benjamin is beginning to enjoy himself, but back on the planet the cops are following Benjamin's last hit and thinking about the fourth. As they try and figure out if there is a pattern and who is Benjamin's next victim. It was a priest who ever was trying to tip him off was going a good job. The cool one had a good system to Benjamin's robot there engineering was similar. I should have mentioned it earlier they both did things when they were commanded. This time h=the hint=am nans d the oxygen was taking the murders more seriously especially this one. They were going to guard the victim the priest. As the priest was just leaving the chapel, all they had to do is approach him, as he closed the doors, oxygen was making an approach not knowing that the man was going to run. The priest was quick, and the oxygen was in grabbing distance it was not long before oxygen had run out of oxygen.
Oxygen:" Boy, that guys quick."
Oxygen fails to make the arrest, he knows not to shout at him as there might be people listening.
The oxygen takes a breath and continues as the hitman with him a full-on chase begins as they are now side by side sprinting down the grave yard and down some wonky paths in to disused fields and back on to the main roads they stop knowing that they had lost him. In the end when they could run no more they both shout out. The priest still does not know that he is a target. As the priest runs off obviously not wanting to talk oxygen opens a discussion and starts a debate he continues that there could have been a hundred reasons why he ran. He continues that he was obviously scared of something. as the priest ran not wanting to talk to the police. Not realizing that he was in danger, he runs in to town which was near there was more people there and it

was easier for him to hide. Ass he stops to gather his breath looking over his shoulder their ws nobody following him yet. He walks in to a clothe s shop looking for some normal clothes. He decides s to by a jacket it was a girl's jacket and it would work whoever was following him was clearly looking for some one wearing black. He then went for dome shoe s grabbing any pair that was different to what he was wearing. Not caring if they fitted or not. Oxygen was right behind him, the priest thought that he had out run them but in fact it was the opposite. The col one was a seriously fast verse. The priest looked like he had been court. As he was pushed in to the super verse he was not happy ensure why they were arresting him. after they had begun to drive the oxygen explains they both try to explain to him that he was in danger, the p [rest opposites for running and he goes into shock when find s out that he is a target a hit. The man asks if he can get out of the car as he claimed to feel sick the oxygen pulls over in a busy street the man get out of the car a ND is sick then with in a second he runs off. The hitman could have seen that move coming it was a classical movie stunt. They are both quick enough to act. They both get out of the cool one and phaser him. The priest falls to the floor in pain and passes out completely.

The two cops pick him up and puts him in side the col one. He is cuff for his own protection.

The man is unsettled and wants answers that the oxygen does not have. In the end he just shuts up not saying anything. They knew that he was going to run off gain and the truth is that they needed him and could use him for bate which was what was happening. The priset wanted something to drink and was asking for a beer. The hitman is persuaded and says yes if it calms him down. Toney both tell him to shut up as he had not stopped talking for an hour.

The oxygen finally gets him calm enough to tell him the truth.
Oxygen:" just shut up and be quiet we have a lot riding on you."
The priest answers. With holy verb and then continues to the pint of throwing the cup and ripping off the toilet seat and chucking at the cell only rot upset himself more. Everybody ib the office at that point tells

him to shut up. The priest passes out at that moment on the cell bed and did not wake up until a few hours later. Only for the fact that he was being slapped awake and did not awake full until a jug of water had been poured upon him. They were back on track least they thought they were. The hitman puts the man back into the car and drive him home. the oxygen believes that he now safe the oxygen leaves his side and are parked within walking distance of the priest.

Meantime the hitman is being followed by the Benjamin and heist getting real close he is right behind him up to his front door. With the oxygen not around the hitman had left himself in a vulnerable position. Benjamin pulls his weapon the hitman was prised Benjamin tells him not to turn around. The hitman quietly asks Benjamin what he wants. Benjamin tells him that he wants him to stop following him around. The hitman taking all his bottle turns a round knowing that he could be killed, but Benjamin was not there. The hitman is in shock and is trying to locate Benjamin he knows not to move at that point but looks real hard into the darkness. The hitman finally calls the brief encounter in and with an hour the oxygen was by his side. They discuss what had happened. The oxygen was telling the hitman that Benjamin could not kill in cold blood why he did not know in all his victims they all the same they had all killed somebody.
After that conversation the hitman started to argue as the thought of having Benjamin behind him tat close was upsetting him. The argument a=was a long one. The oxygen was on the receiving end of it. The hitman tells oxygen he could have been shot the hitman continues the hitman was quizzed n why Benjamin did not kill him.

The hitman replies that that he was a wanted criminal and heed did not kill him did the oxygen understand. The hitman had no more answers for the moment. Then suggested that his partner the oxygen had been brain washed the oxygen was extremely un happy about what his partner had said they brawl for a minute of=r two the hitman coming in second place as the oxygen would not release him from a head lock until he gave him an apology

Oxygen:" is that it you're going to give in just like that for a treat so what it is part of the job."

The hitman was scared for the first time. Oxygen could finally see it. in the end the two cops part oxygen tell the hitman that he will see him tomorrow and what ever happened this evening was over and done. The hitman closes his door and the oxygen in the cool one slams his shut tight. It was not a good idea to leave the hitman on his own, so the oxygen pulls up down the road and turns the cool one around facing the hitman's house making sue=re that he is safe for the rest of the night.

Benjamin was busy looking for the priest he had already scoped the whole town out thinking that he went some where busy he was on the right tracks the priest was back at his home and Benjamin found him again purely by chance. As he was following his trail he had no idea that he was going to bump straight in to the man meanwhile the hitman still trying to gr=et over the other night and at this time had no concern for the priest.

Benjamin:" hay nice clothes."

The priest:" yeah reasonable."

They look at each other. They both realize that there is something familiar about the situation.

The priest:" do I know you."

Benjamin:" no I do not believe that we have met."

Benjamin knows exactly who he was talking to and shortly after the priest knew too Benjamin did not make the hit straight away, but it was only a matter of time. Just as beaming had disappeared in to the crowed of shoppers the hitman turns up the priest at that point gave the hitman Benjamin's directions. The hitman also goes in to the crowed.

In the end Benjamin stops and turns around he can clearly see the hitman Benjamin shout at him telling him to raise his weapon. The hitman understands him as the people depart making a small lie down the middle of the street people either side of them. Benjamin tells the hitman not to take him for a fool and tells him to go for his gun. The hitman takes another step forward Benjamin is watching the priest is getting excited. As he is speaking to Benjamin steadying his hand. Benjamin knows now that he has been found. He does not take prisoners they both step out in the street. Exciting the people around them even more including the priest. It was a duel. Benjamin has the upper hand as he could morph. The hitman did not waist anytime he fire s first lucky for brinkman that he had only hit his badge. It was enough pressure to force Benjamin off his feet and on to his back. As Benjamin get up he morphed into a tiger. The hitman does not see him coming he was that fast.

Benjamin is happy to continue the hitman does not believe what he is seeing. As he has nonknowledge of the badge Benjamin morphs himself back into himself. The hitman ire's another shot as he pushes the priest over to get him out of the way, so he cannot be harmed fires another shot again not forgetting that he was not the target, but the priest was. As the hitman's shots miss as he falls backwards on to the floor unloading his cartage until it is empty. Giving Benjamin a chance to get on top off him the hitman believes that he going to die and closes his eyes Benjamin sees the priest the real target morphing himself back raises his phaser and shoots the priest dead. The dead body falls to the floor. Benjamin knows that the job was done, the people gather around the cop and the priest in silence and shock. Benjamin is on his way home again.

The priest was dead, and the hitman was alive Benjamin tells his robot it should have been the other way around.
The last three targets that Benjamin was thinking about even before he praised the dead priest had come into mind. They would not be easy. It

felt weird to walk on planet earth as within a few hundred yeas it would not be here. It might be destroyed. The earthlings did not have the technology.as I walked from street to street I eventually found my space ship. Benjamin was happy to greet on board. This time I took it up above the planet and hovered there in and above the clouds. Benjamin fell asleep fast and his robot was in control and the next morning he awoke me. as I was waking up asked the computer for the facts. It put them in front of me on my computer screen. I could clearly see everything that I had done. After I was trying not to think about it to much.
Benjamin is happy to continue.

CHAPTER THIRTEEN
IT TAKE TWO TO TANGO

I was fresh out of ideas I had just met the man who was going to end my life I di not know why I did not kill him myself. I guess it takes two to tango, the priest target was dead I was wondering when it would be my turn. I was feeling very little remorse over the targets position I was glad that he was dead. Benjamin was still getting to terms of the in and the outs of his job. He also knows that he is being used. He was like the robot with no real feeling. He knows that he is being used as a machine. Benjamin flees to the bottom of the ocean knowing that his feminise are still up there.

END OF PART ONE

Spirit 5
The Beginning
INTRODUCTION

I have created four super human characters the first is Benjamin and he is the spirit five, an assassin from the world that looks over the planet earth. How I created him, I guess it was through the thought though my mind the idea was that he was to eliminate seven extremely important people who had miss used their judgement and powers governing the planet earth they were to be punished. As every superhero has a story there is a good part and a bad part one minute he would be doing things for the good and other times he would be doing thing for the bad. The hero in this story is all bad in his case the bad guys win and there is a curse to go with it as Benjamin must live with the five super powers that process him. In this case it is the same, but there is a story to it.

I do not know how I came about it, one minute I was sitting there on my stool writing in the dark the next minute I had created him Benjamin. Benjamin is the spirit. On top of this I had some more characters that I had created. I decided at the time that the story needed a bit of help, so I decided to add a couple of futuristic coppers called the oxygen and the hitman and gave them a car called the cool one, after the number plate which was private on their car, Benjamin is close to it as it is close to the public. They do not like it, there must be bad guys in the story and there both it. not forgetting the real master, the silhouette, a sassy cool individual and killer that brings Benjamin down a good looking cool adversary that has the power to bring the Benjamin down he that bad guy in the story. Who will win, who knows yet have a read.

As I continue, Benjamin knows that there is something going on in planet earth and that's the only reason that he is there. Benjamin has some help from his friends a robot that we call a robot some of the time and other time's we call him mar arty and a couple of crazy sun flowers called the flowers to guide him.

Preface

Benjamin knows that there is something wrong on the planet earth the story go's he is busy moving to a new house he is upstairs in his attic. As he clears the boxes in his attic he stumbles getting ready to move he stubbles across an old tin at first, he ignores it but the feeling that the tin gave him drew him back to it, so he puts it aside for another time except he is drawn to it more the more he tries to disregard the thought the more his mind thinks about it. he is extremely drawn to it. as the next few days past looking at the box he decides to open it and when he doe's he finds a magic badge. This badge is extremely special and once it is on you it cannot be removed from the clothing and will slowly become part of the body. Benjamin does not know this at first, Benjamin decides to fly to Britain to a professor to find the meaning of the badge and wants to know what exactly what it's purpose.

Spirit five

THE BEGINING
Chapter one

It was the lion that praises before it makes a kill, I had to make seven hits on planet earth. The first was a business man the second was a holy man and the third was a position. I came from OutSpace another planet and I was obeying my orders. I was blessed with five super human powers hence the badge that I was wearing, I was told to use the badge as a weapon and away of escape if I got in to trouble. I was not the good guy in this war, I was a killer, I was the assassin, the ultimate weapon. As I sat down in my arm chair in my space craft thirty thousand feet below the Atlantic Ocean, I was deep in thought over the thought of how I was going to make the first move in fact in the end it was going to be the other way around. I had forgotten to put the ship in stealth I was pick up on the radar of a us vasal a submarine two in fact. These people do not mess around and I was thinking I should blow them out of the water. I got the message

CAPTAIN: "we have an undefinable object on our radars precede code red."

OFFICER: "Ready when you are sir."

CAPTAIN: "Send a message of peace to them whoever they are remind them that they are in our waters."

OFFICER: "Okay captain."

Benjamin calls for his robot from out the back of his ship, he is busy watering the flowers

BENJAMIN: "Yes I did, keep the u boat company while I decide what to do."

Before Benjamin has a chance to think the robot butts in.

THE ROBOT: "According to my calculations we have three options the first is to attack them the second we can surface which will only cause a stand by and the third we can stay put there is a sixty percent chance of getting away if our stealth is working, they will not pick us up on their radar and we could float right by."

BENJAMIN: "That is a lot of words for a robot. Give me some therapy."

THE ROBOT: "Well of course we are both nuts."

The robot continues: "Energy levels are low we are not going to make it as the oxygen levels are to low also I am sorry to say Benjamin that we have no choice but to surface."

BENJAMIN: "I hope your right okay send her up."
THE ROBOT: "Hay man I do not make mistakes."
BENJAMIN: "Take her up to the top."

In the back ground the two sun flowers are discussing the incident.
SUNFLOWER ONE: "Were going on an adventure."
SUN FLOWER TWO: "no we are not we are surfacing."
SUNFLOWER ONE:" It is still an adventure."
Benjamin takes control of the vesicle taking his machine up two thousand meters fast knowing that the two trident submarines would be waiting for him at the top of the ocean and would follow him.
As Benjamin slowly rises and out of the water's surface his space ship sits in-between the two subs.

With both submarine s by his sides he is hailed by them both captain s, the first stands on board and tries to make contact Benjamin refuses to answer, as he is hailed again he can feel the pressure as he is watching more and more soldiers appear on the subs decks either side of Benjamin and armed the commandos are called to their bridge signalling each other. Benjamin spacecraft is just hovering above the sea level, with no cause of action the submarine on the right side of him opens fire sending the submarine on the left side of Benjamin and his space ship in to chaos. There soldiers shouting and bumping each other off their submarines and into the oceans, there was an array of missiles which were sent to the spacecraft soon afterwards, Benjamin speaks to his systems.

BENJAMIN: "Vertical systems position computer. Hold tight".

The computer confers its orders and quickly becomes vertically up right within a few seconds it launches itself up into the hemisphere, a cool escape. Benjamin thinks so.

THE COMMANDER: "Well I have never seen anything like that before."

The submarines return to the underneath of the ocean.

CHAPTER TWO

TWENTY-FOUR HOURS AWAY

Benjamin is back in space about twenty-four hours away from his target. Zero gravity, as he floats around his space ship fixing things, it's damage and thinking how he was going to do the dirty work ahead of him. As he floats towards his computer and sitting down turning the system on the flicks through the video footage, images and looking hard at them and planning how he was going to meet the first target, how he would approach him on the earth to make the kill.

Benjamin did not know that the British fleet that he meet had been filming him and within a few days of the incident it was all over the news and all over the world. There was headline s such as alien vasal surfaces and other quotes the earth has been invaded and unidentified spaceship harbours sea and other stuff like naval officer's sink after seeing mysterious ship found at sea and so on. Benjamin knew that it was now a silly time to approach the planet again at this time and if it was not for the ships damage he would have made the hit sooner. He had only had a few hours to make it back to the earth. Benjamin was thinking that he was going to miss the hit all together the targets time to die was only a few hours away.

It had to be timed perfection, Benjamin knew this he had too there was a time on everything that he did on that day it had a purpose a meaning and he knew that he would only get one chance, he could not afford to miss it. as the hours turned into minutes he was going to attempt the approach to planet earth.

BENJAMIN: "Give me a visual on planet earth please."

He speaks to his computer

BENJAMIN: "Visual. Visual recovered scan area for required address and home destination.

We are on our way."

Benjamin slowly takes control of the space ship pushing a few buttons here and there and a few switches taking control of the spaceship. Taking it to the earth and planet.

BENJAMIN: "What's the time please."

THE ROBOT: "It is exactly five minutes to twelve o'clock in the evening."

Benjamin only had five minutes to find him the clock was ticking fast Benjamin tells his computer to go to hyper speed stealth they were at the target in a jiffy.

A few second s later Benjamin sees his target and the game was on. Benjamin was waiting for the weather change it was by god that the weather would work on my behalf. As I approached the planet earth I got lower it was a rough landing as the weather as I said changed rapidly too hot to cold with a long dark sky to go with it. it was getting cloudier and it had begun to rain. By the time that I had settled the ship down I was ready for the target. The target that I had not mentioned until now was of significant important it was the mayor of the city of angles, LA. I have been there before and have fond memories as I landed the ship, the ship had a heat sensor scanning device infer red to scan the building for the target within a few minutes I had found him. I was watching him, but I had company which I knew as my robot had my back.
THE ROBOT: "Five you have company. There's a verse in the ally way beside of you with the words COOL ONE on the number plate do you recognise it."
BENJAMIN: "No I do not."
THE ROBOT:" I| have tried the profile but I am getting nothing."
Benjamin replies that is now aware and is moving in on the target and he is content on hunting down the mayor.
The robot's instinct is being to tell Benjamin not to make the move, but Benjamin refuses to listen he says it is too close and wants his target.

It did not take too long for the cool one to find Benjamin systems and they were both on to him that's the hitman and the oxygen. Benjamin ship was now on the ground with not a lot of room to manuver. Benjamin watches intensively the two cops sitting in their cool one but not as cool as a space ship benjamin says to himself. Oxygen undoes the window as he smokes a cigarette.
HITMAN: "Do you know that really stinks."
OXYGEN: "I heard it was really bad for you. Your breath too. "
HITMAN: "Yeah well do not tell the wife. You must have a really sweet kiss."
OXYGEN: "Is this our guy."
HITMAN: "Probably he looks like the disruption, he looks like he has just cloaked his ship."
OXYGEN:" I think that we should give him a welcome."
Benjamin heard the whole conversation, he continues to his computer.
BENJAMIN: "Computer arm rockets on target and full shields."
The cool one's car was also armoured also Benjamin takes a chance and at the last second that the target had changed. Benjamin is in two minds he knows that the real target is the mayor, but the two cool coppers were on their way also just for being in the wrong place at the wrong time.
Benjamin knows that he has been seen and must make a split decision, he must decide if he should make the first move he is communicating with his robot who is on his space ship for a quick report on the situation the robots reply ids that he has a fifty/ fifty chance of reaching his targets now that there are three of them. It was clear to Benjamin that the cool one and its passengers were in Benjamin's way. Benjamin could not kill in cold blood there had to be a reason but however if the cool one made the first move. By the laws of Benjamin's planet, he could put it through his council, and defend himself. It would be by luck if the two cops made the first move in fact they were probably thinking the same as him. There was a long silence within Benjamin as he study's them form a distance knowing that they could not see him.
Benjamin speaks to his robot.

BENJAMIN: "Am I clear."
THE ROBOT:" No you have company and it looks like you have a lot it. There is car parked about two hundred feet from you over the voice indicator it sound s like the cops and above you a helicopter and it looks like some cops on the street are approaching you."
Benjamin says to himself that he can do it even though he thinks that the target has too much cover then changes his mind. And says to himself that he thinks that he should go. Benjamin loses the first round. Not thinking he believes that he has lost until he receives a message about the badge he had totally forgot even so now it was too late he was uncertain, and he just wanted to get out of and off the streets, but his consciousness kept on telling him to use the badge.
BENJAMIN:" How stupid is this this is useless it's not going to work."
CONSIOUSNESS: "Use the badge. You have to believe."

BENJAMIN: "This is rubbish I prefer the old-fashioned way, you know guns at dawn and all the other stuff. So, what do you want me to do step inside the future."
CONSIOUSNESS. "It is your future."
Benjamin stops for a second as he is now back on the space craft as he walks on he walks back off almost straight away.
BENJAMIN: "I'm going outside and I'm going to nail this guy. Open the doors."
Benjamin welding his space gun leaves the ship walking like an assassin would walk he heads towards the building, he already knows who the target is all he needs to know is where his target is in the building. Benjamin has not already got use to his badge or the gun as they are gifts, but he knew deep down inside that he would use his new powers wisely and it would take time to perfect them and he would have to sue them in the end if he wanted to survive in the end.
Benjamin walks into the office building as he pushes the door open the cool one down the street tells the oxygen that the building has company as an armed man has entered the building. Benjamin already knows that he has been seen and takes the chance that he could make the hit there are people everywhere Benjamin speaks to his robot telling him that he is well protected as he continues to look for the target. The robot tells Benjamin to press his badge a couple of times

Benjamin tells him that he is sound with his gun, but the robot overrides his mission and tells him to hurry up and press the badge, finally Benjamin listens as he presses the spirit five badge twice he changes in to a tiger he changes quickly in to the forces beast. The people in the building were just standing watching him as he moved through the people some pointing other running to get out of his way as this is happening fast the cool one and the two cops turn up you would think in the nick of time, but they were too late also.
OXYGEN: "Guns out, time to party."
Oxygen draws first trying to get a scope on the tiger who was Benjamin, Oxygen is also speaking to the hitman who in touch with the cool one just outside the building. Benjamin knows that the two cops mean business too, he morphs back to his human form as the people innocent people all leave the building as they were allowed Benjamin makes his way up stairs to the mayor's office the two cops are following him. The mayor was an easy target. When Benjamin walked into the office the mayor was sitting at his desk. He spoke quietly.
THE MAYOR:" I knew that you were coming."
As the mayor took another line of the substance that he was putting up his nose he continues.
THE MAYOR: "What did I do."
I could tell he was sorry, but I was not there to play god, I was not the person to do the forgiving all I could say was to him was that it was not man who has the power to forgive that was god. I looked at him once more as he took another line through a note it looked to me if he was trying to OD before I filled him with bullets. I could hear the engine of the cool one just outside I knew that I would have some company on the way out. And I also knew that the two cops were heading my way. I suppose I could call it gods victim.

BENJAMIN:" Hard luck your dead."
Benjamin pulls his gun out of his holster and with cause of concern puts a couple of bullets in him two to the chest he was dead. Benjamin did not need to leave a calling card. He thinks that the police would get the message. The power of Benjamin's gun went right through him and the window four feet behind him the sound echoed through the walls of the building, giving the two cops Benjamin's where about. Benjamin was clever enough to figure out the rest he leaps over the body of the dead guy, the mayor and out of the shattered window as

the cops enter the room landing on top of the three-parked private numbered police car. He makes a smooth landing as he uncloaks his space ship and makes it back on foot. Benjamin speaks to himself saying the old-fashioned phase one down six to go. He continues talking to himself trying to explain to himself what he had done he was feeling high it was bit of a buzz. He continued that the fall from the window was incredible, he had made it back to his space ship and was still talking about the experience

BENJAMIN: "That was a hundred-foot drop. I do not know how I did it, but I did it, has to be this space costume."

The robot butts in.

ROBOT: "It is not a costume it is a suit, wear it with pride, you're the spirit five."

The robot continues: "It is made of in destructible material through the badge."

Mean time while Benjamin is back on his space ship looking for some fresh air and taking a breather from his life the two coppers are weighing up the pro s and cons off the maximum carnage of what the spirit five had left behind.

OXYGEN: "We've missed him he's long gone with a smile on his face."

HITMAN: "I'm going to call it in maybe somebody out there might had seen something."

OXYGEN:" This guy in front of me is dead he is the mayor, why him?

HITMAN: "I do not know are the drugs on the table his or is this a set up

OXYGEN: "I'll run it through forensic, it looks to me like murder two bullets to the chest."

HITMAN: "Is there anything else."

OXYGEN: "Two shots unregistered gun two bullets to the chest."

HITMAN: "We should have waited how did he escape."

OXYGEN:" No, we should have waited, how did he escape."

HITMAN:" It looked like he jumped out of the window after he but a couple of bullets through it."

OXYGEN: I'll take some photographs you go down stairs and see if he's has left another mess."

HITMAN: "OKAY."

OXYGEN: "Oh and call the medics and tell them to come and collect this they have got a mess on their hands."

Benjamin before that conversation was boasting how somehow, he miraculously landed on his feet after the large leap on to his space craft. He rolled onto his feet, he orders marri arty the robot to open the cargo doors and steps upon the ship.

BENJAMIN: "Job done."

MARRIARTY: "Yes job done, let's get out of here "

Benjamin walks through the spaceship to his cockpit, he shows no remorse as for what just happened as it was by order of the council he buckles up sitting in his space chair and leaves the planet only to know that he would be back and does not know that the two cops and the cool one will be waiting for him or even more so that they had been watching. He was now a target the hunter becoming the hunted.

CHAPTER THREE
THE REVERSE

For the killing of the mayor la that's loss angles the city of angles Benjamin is offered by his councils some time off. As he is standing in front of the council and is questioned. The council needed all the information all the details of what had just taken place on the planet earth. As they insisted that everything they do is by god as the planet is by god but not the earth they have different rules.

The first councillor starts the discussion

FRIST COUNCILLOR ANTHONY: "how did you do it."?

BENJAMIN:" I used the suit."

SECOND COUNTCILLOR ANTHONY: "When did you make contact."?

They had to make that everything that I did was done was done by their law in a way that binds them to their law.

BENJAMIN: "Of I did he was snuffing something up his nose he was stuffing his face with narcotics it was obvious he knew that I was on my way to him."

COUNTCILLOR ANDREW: "What was said."?

BENJAMIN: Not a lot by the time I had got there up in the mayor's room the cops had picked up my signal through their car apparently called the cool one that's what I hear through the grape vine. It has good technology but not advanced as ours I was making my way upstairs."

As Benjamin spoke he was slowly beginning to feel out of place with the questioning' it was like he was on trial and not the victim on trial which he was unsettling. He had no choice but to continue.

BENJAMIN: "Everything that I did on that day was by your law. I played by your rules and know you bring me here. M y robot has video footage of my every move, you have nothing on me or my crew. My robot has recorded everything that has happened if you do not believe in me then turn to my computer the evidence will be the same as I have just spoke. I was doing my job."

MARRIERTY: "I have to agree."

Benjamin continues:" I found the target which was the mayor of New York, as requested and I ill mated him as requested I killed him like I was ordered. The worlds a better place."

COUNTCILLOR ANDREW: "Did you speak to the victim."?

BENJAMIN: "No I played him two bullets to the chest as my computer ordered."

COUNTCILLOR ANTHONY:" What happened when you first entered the building."?

Benjamin is beginning to feel uneasy about the questioning, but he continues to answer their questions.
BENJAMIN: "There was lots of people around mainly a lot of office workers, at that point I had to use my badge and I morphed into a tiger by touching my badge to scare them aside, I then morphed again changing myself back to my human form by thinking about it through my mind."
The badge being controlled by my robot also inside the space ship.
COUNTCILLOR ANDERW: "Well it seems that you have done everything within yours powers and gift to up hold our law you are free to go for your next mission."
Benjamin bows his head and leaves the court rooms and leaves the council. He feels ashamed, the robot understood the way Benjamin was feeling and comforts him knowing that they would have to come back soon.
Benjamin had caught on he knew by the way he was being questioned that it was a game in their eyes a game that Benjamin was willing to play which they did not know, Benjamin from that point would trust nobody. Even though Benjamin wanted to shout at anything and everything through the pressure of the court room he broke when he got to his quarters.
It seemed to Benjamin that everything had revised he did not know whether it was there game or whether it was his mind. The death of the mayor was defiantly being playing on his mind and playing on his consciousness. The whole journey through the council all the questions after questions after questions it was like being a Ginny pig. There was something going on upstairs not upstairs in my mind but in theirs.
Benjamin knew that there was something up, but he chose to ignore it that was Benjamin to a tee. It was like him to ignore his problems if they insisted and would wait for them to pilfered up and deal with them later. He chose to ignore them for now. It was like the reversed had happened Benjamin was busy putting his thoughts beside with ease they meant nothing for now. All he wanted was a beer and a smoke. There was a knock at my quarters doors Benjamin did not want to answer it. but it was instinct that made him walk to the door.

Benjamin opens the door, to his surprise it was personal. A conversation started. And there was an officer with him.
PERSONAL:" Hello."
BENJAMIN:" Hello, come in."
OFFICER: "We have been asked to give you this."
It was a badge the same badge that I was wearing on my suit it was the same badge that I was being offered to my robot we were going back to court this time my robot was on trial for an award.
COUNTCILLOR ANDREW: "Well it seems to me that you have done all you could have done to except and obey your orders you also are ready and free to go to your next mission."
"You are free to go."
The officer hand s Benjamin his next mission in an envelope in the envelope was his orders Benjamin thanks the officer for nothing and sends him on his way. Benjamin waits until the officer is at a distant and then opens the envelope in private but does not look at it. He closes the room door so that he has privacy.
In the envelope was the next job he looks at it hard thinking about what is in it. he takes she eve elope and puts it down on a table in the room, close to his bunk. It was a message from the court hearing this afternoon well that's what he thought. Benjamin was clearly in a bed mood a few minutes later senator Simon was to call upon him.
CENETOR SIMON: "Benjamin are you okay."
BENJAMIN: "Yeah I'm fine, just a little out of touch now due to the hearing, it has not sunk in just yet."
CENETOR SIMON:" It's not just the killing it's a mission you're the very best, probably the best in our world. You know already that you have been chosen to help their world to help mankind there are a lot of misguided people out there in our system. You nerve being employed to stop them do you understand."
BENAJMIN: I'm not sure that I do understand after the hearing today one second I'm doing right the next I'm doing wrong.
SENETOR SIMON:" You do not have to feel that way." What you are feeling Benjamin is the reverse it is like everything that you have ever experience after a battle it is the opposite experience of e=what you are thinking, what you feel, what you see. it might take you a few days to understand it so get some rest".
Benjamin did not know what exactly the senator Simon was saying and again it seemed that their whole programme was the reverse of what benjamin was saying and thinking. Everything that I said to the

council had reflected on him, it was very personal. There was a lot of pressure, but rule s were rules. And the whole court room seemed to be on the mayor's side. I was doing them a favour and it was like they were trying to twist everything I said at that point. Something was wrong not just in our council but on the planet. I did not find time to find the answer or the knowledge to understand it at this point, so I put it aside. I decided to play their game until I had more of an insight of what was going on and what I really wanted I was thinking that I was being used the thought was now that I was the target and I was going to be the hunted.

It was early morning after a good night of no sleep as I tossed and turned on my bunk half a wake and half asleep as I was heading out of my mind for some proper sleep I knew deep down that I was not going to get the rest I needed, and I knew that the only rest that I knew that I was going to get was on my own ship. As I adjusted my pillow over ten times within an hour, but I was still uncomfortable and at eased but in the end, I gave up I had to do something, and it was a smoke a cigarette. As I pushed it into my mouth and breathed the smoke out into the fresh air. I felt a little better, but I knew also that the feeling would not last, I needed to get away, but I had a contract to full fill. As I opened the eve elope there was three hundred thousand credits in it in space terms that's a lot of loot unfortunately for me it was a dream as I was asleep in the real envelope was the second job the second hit the man that I was going to kill. The next man was a priest a holy man what he had done I do not know I was not in the business of hanging around business that was not my business. His name was father frank I began to look at his profile early it said everything in the document in the envelope I had taken the letter out of its envelope.

I was back in the space ship this priest according to the court was being totally out of terms with his own spiritually by pushing the things that he preached was causing our planet and his world in to chaos. He had to be stopped, he was known to over express himself and sucking the life out of the people that wanted to understand but did not understand. I guess in a sense that he had gone a little over the top. It could have been a little nicer. Anyway, I Had a job to do and I had got compile to the letter what was in the envelope. I was heading back to the planet earth again.

The only problem this time was as it was calculated as I sat in the space chair in my cockpit. As I zoomed through the earth's atmosphere with my robot taking the control of the ship as I went to lie down and its crazy sunflowers for company we were going to make a hit in the day time. When I awoke I spoke to mar arty he gave me the priests exact coordinates as we landed just outside his church. I felt uneasy something was wrong. I went to my computer.

BENJAMIN: "Hay, computer you hailed me. What's up".

COMPUTER: "You seem to have a rival as there is already a hit on this man".

BENJAMIN: "What does this mean".

COMPUTER: We have two options, one you can full fill your orders and kill the priest or two you could kill the priest and then kill the hitman".

BENJAMIN: "What would be the outcome if I killed them both".

COMPUTER: "Good question I will have an answer for you in a second I am just going to send a message home".

Benjamin waits a few minutes on his toes in trepidation. The computer gives Benjamin an answer he tells Benjamin that he has permission to remove both if he can the hitman and now the priest were both going to die.

BENJAMIN:" Good."

Benjamin walks out of his space ship there are holy people everywhere, he knows he cannot touch them as they were who they were. He reaches into his pushing a button to close the visor down, so he is masked. Just as he nears his victim two motor bukes near him he finds the second hit the man on the motor cycle lifts his gun Benjamin can see it quite clearly. The man on the bike lifts his gun and fires maybe a round or two Benjamin attempts to take them out he lifts his gun and sends an array of bullets hitting the motor cycle at first them of Couse hitting the rider with nobody to control the bike the assign on the back was all left for dead as the bike crashes in as few on coming verses. There was a burst of flames but however Benjamin did not have enough time to go after them or even see if they alive or dead his real target now was the priest and after everything that just happened it made things a little easier as now there were just people watching the blaze of fire and smoke. Benjamin continues to walk into the building there are some guards by the targets doors before he can reach the priest he will have to remove the guards. The guards pick up Benjamin extremely fast they both came at him at once. It did not make things any easier as some of the crowd was now beginning to disperse Benjamin uses his helmet to get a picture of the priested helmet was computerised it locks on to his target Benjamin takes out the targets one by one until there was nobody left to guard the priest.

The priest did not see Benjamin coming, as he stood in the room full of his dead body guards he falls to his knees. Benjamin see no remorse. He pulls his gun out of his space suit.

BENJAMIN: "Any last requests."

The priest does not answer as Benjamin raises his arm. The priest is dead Benjamin's job for now is done the second target on his list has been assisted. Benjamin had put a few bullets through his head. He leaves the building calmly walking past people until he gets outside and calls upon his robot to send the space ship. As his ship arrives the cops turn up just a minute behind him that would be the oxygen and the hitman. Benjamin has no more time to play games.

Benjamin is in his cockpit making a getaway while he takes his space ship up more and more coppers are turning up.

As Benjamin is safely back on board the spirit, he has time to figure out the power of his badge he was not looking to confident. Benjamin tells his computer to go to stealth, as soon as the ship does Benjamin is out of there site of the authority's, he makes his escape.

The two cops were sitting just outside of the building while his cars computer is organizing the lock down of the area, so they can start the forensic proceedings. Just on the edge deciding if they should enter the scene of the crime they had no business there at that point as another team beat them to it. they discussed it for a minute or two. Between them and their boss who was on the end of the phone they both were being told no. they decide to go in to the building despite what they were told.

THE HITMAN: "Let's go in."

THE OXYGEN: I" do not know what I am doing I do think that this is a good idea."

THE HITMAN:" come on it will be an adventure. You might learn something."

THE OXYGEN: "We are going to be taken by the scuffs of our colours I bet I lose my badge. I will blame you."

The two cops both get out of the cool one they call it the cool one because it's on its number plates.

They enter the reception as the forensic team are looking at things and trying to figure it out. The two-start looking at things two until they bump in the three-opposing team and told to leave the scene there was a small conversation to go with the orders.

Benjamin was on his way back home to tell his council that the job had been done.

Back in the office block the two cops are hailed back to the scene and are welcomed to have a look around. The local authorities did not want the cops there, any of them. they were part of the evidence and were going to be questioned.

CHIEF: "Okay what are you too boys doing out of your jurisdiction."

The two cops did not answer they both knew that if they gave such as a twitch the chief would kick off and shout at them extremely loud. They did not want to tell the chief that they were looking for a space ship and an alien got go with it.

They did not want to tell him that they were slowly hunting a space killing hitman.

THE HITMAN: "Look it is just following portico were just gathering a few facts."

THE OXYGEN:" we were down stairs in the area, in the car we heard gun fire."

CHIEF: "do you expect me to believe that did you to know that you could be arrested for a breech interfering with police business."

THE HITMAN:" I think we should tell him"

THE OXYGEN:" No I do not the guys crazy let's get out of here, honestly do we look like the police yeah I think so what could he not see."

The two cops decide to walk out.

They both leave the scene heading back to the verse the cool one.
THE OXYGEN: "That was close a little bit too close for my likening. Come on get in what I did not like is what I just saw it is the kind of mess that you can never get out of your head. Do I get paid for that because if I do I'm going to ask for a pay rise?"
THE HITMAN: "Probably not but we could ask."
Benjamin is back in space or there about, he knows that he's got away with it. The first and now the second he sends us a message to his planet telling the council that the second job is done. He gets no reply. Knowing that his council had got the message he thinks that he is being respected and they were letting rest.
Benjamin closes his eye's the thought of killing did not leave a great impression on the mind. He was trying to find the save in his head because it was a recurring thought and that was the problem. But however, he knew the feeling would subside but right now he was mourning.

Benjamin closes his eyes again, he knows that he is safe but how safe was the question? after the work is done who knows what Benjamin future will be. After an hour or so he opens his eyes the voice of a friend his robot mar arty wakes him.
MARARTY: "Welcome back."
BENJAMIN: "Thank you that was a seriously rough ride, where are we."
MARARTY: "Are you okay."
BENJAMIN: "Yes I am."
MARARTY:" Did you use the badge."
BENJAMIN: "I cannot remember."
Benjamin tries to account but his mind is blank. He thinks even harder until he receives it he continues yes, I remember I was a tiger and I clawed some guy to death.
MARARTY: "Close, you shot him."
BENJAMIN: "That does not make me feel any better."
MARARTY: "You chose to remember, you did not have to."
Well I guess the badge works.

MARARATY: "Do you know what the rest does."
BENJAMIN: "No I have not had the chance to use it yet."
MARARTY:" Would you like me to help you understand it."
BENJAMIN: "Not right now we can do it another time. I need to recover I need to wake up maybe later."
As Benjamin closes his eyes again he drifts off again. Mar arty agrees he should be resting. And tells him to go back to sleep. As Benjamin as Benjamin slowly falls asleep he's dreaming of his next hit. This time it was the mayor of New York. As he dreams as in any dream before he awakes and misses the outcome he must improvise. He knows part of the future this time he awakes suddenly with the sweat to go with it, falling off his bed on to the floor and stays there still half confused award half conscious and still half asleep

Mar arty turns the gravity on using it slowly to lift Benjamin back on his bunk as his body slowly rises upwards floating the robot slowly pushes him back on to the bunk and straps him down. Mara arty puts some music on he's into classical. His two other friends the two sunflowers are still asleep also the robot is left alone while playing the music he is talking the computer to keep himself entertained. While the robot is looking after the space ship. While everybody is asleep the robot decides if he should take the space back down to planet earth. He decides that he would wait for Benjamin to awake instead. The robot was scared for Benjamin he was the robots best friend the robot watches the two sun flowers they had awoke by the music and had started to sing along with it. cheering the robot out of its worries. The robot sets up the coordinates to take Benjamin back to his home planet.as the sun flowers were in the back-ground singing soul lyrics to classical music mar arty joins in the flowers were fun to be with once you had got to know them. As mar arty sings with the sun flowers Benjamín slowly awakes finally feeling like his old self but in a temper, that was the price you pay for killing. He did not know what was to come he did not know that being a killer was a disease. As he undoes the straps that have him locked down he floats gently around to his cockpit

Checking messages and making sure that they were not being followed. As the earth did not have the technology to follow Benjamín waits in silence now for the next orders of the destination of his next target will be they were off to New York in a few days.

Two days had past and Benjamín had received nothing he wanted to go back to the earth there was something about that planet that he was drawn to. Benjamin closes his eyes but only for a moment he was thinking why does the silhouette want to destroy this planet

May be Benjamín thinks as he enters his dream.

Benjamin dreams of the planet earth things start to look dark at first. He was dreaming of peace but for some strange reason that he does not know, things take a shape and things take change. Add the dream becomes darkness. There's destruction and then Benjamín suddenly awakes, not knowing what the dream was about Benjamín wants to go back to the earth as he was in love way=the what he saw in his dreams. He turns to his robot mar arty.
BENJAMIN: "Bring me some pitchers of the planet earth."
MARARTY: "The planet earth."
BENJAMIN: "Yes."
Mar arty turn to a big screen basically the ships ships cockpit window and asks Benjamín again just to make sure what he wants.
It seems to Benjamín with the knowledge in front of him that the earth is smaller than the moon and even smaller the sun and even smaller the Benjamin's home planet.
MARARTY: "The earth is still a big place."

Even so the planet earth had been abused by humans Benjamín plugs himself in to the robot and then in to the computer on his deck side dashboard. Benjamin down loads all the knowledge of the planet to himself. Mar arty does and within twelve hours Benjamín has all the knowledge of the earth that man has recorded to date. When he has finished he does not know that he has overloaded his brain with the knowledge. Being an alien and not human he passes out, but he now knows everything while he sleeps. As he sleeps the knowledge of the earth rips through him with even its future he falls father into a deeper sleep. and has uncontrollable fits as his brain fights the power of it. the knowledge and the power of was taking over Benjamín as he falls even in to a deeper sleep.

His robot is confused and is worried about Benjamin he had not woken yet, and it had been a few days the two flowers plants were put close to him they might annoy him back from where ever he was. They were all ways being noisy it was just an idea. But it was a good idea at the time although it did not work.
FLOWER 1: "Do you think that he will awake."
FLOWER 2:" he will come around eventually."
FLOWER 1: "he has been life less for days."
FLOWER 2:" two days."
FLOWER 1: "let's sing a song it might help. Like some soul music."
FLOWER 2: "I do not think that will work but we can try."
The flower s burst in a song and there dancing and shouting in hope that Benjamín come back he does not wake up.
Benjamin is still in the deep sleep dreaming but this time he is dreaming od =f the next hit which meant that he was on his way back. When Benjamín awake all, he could say was the words." Bad people come first."

Mar arty thinks that the badge is to power full for Benjamin to weld and tries to remove it in hope that he would wake up but the badge un known to the robot will never come off. Every time he does try the badge grows stronger. The power was also within Benjamin, mar arty is confused Benjamin knows. The two cops in the cool one is also thinking about Benjamin the deep sleep that Benjamin was blocking their thoughts the power off the sound of Benjamin in his sleep was dealing for both cops as they both clasps their head in pain that the sound was so powerful windows in buildings that Benjamin had been in would crack an explode. As Benjamin slowly dreams he his arm slowly move s up to his chest and he presses the badge unconsciously. On this occasion nothing happens the robot is concerned as his actions are simultaneous he had done these two or three times within a couple of hours. Benjamin cannot stop repeating the term spirit. Huis happen every hour in to the morning the robot=get thinks that the job is to tough and wants Benjamín to bow out. But he has no way of telling him. The robot has run out of ideas and goes for a recharge.

CHAPTER FOUR

MOVIE BREAKDOWN

When Benjamín finally woke up it was like the end of the movie, tears from everybody including the welcoming by the flowers. It was amazing how much his three companions cared and how much the sleep effects Benjamin's mind. With a moment Benjamín whole personality changed. He moved differently and spoke differently, it was obvious there was a change in his whole personality there was something new about him. Mar arty took a second to think that it was cool Benjamín had not noticed it as much as his friends on the spaceship. The flowers did not even notice, and they notice everything, they caught on in the end. In all the confusion Benjamín was also receiving his orders and was glad that he would be returning to the planet earth. He seemed to think that it was a good place to be his friend s thought differently.

Benjamin: "let's go to New York."

Mar arty: "I'm just plugging in the coordinates now. We have one hour and two minutes hyper speed

Benjamin was on his seconded hit the mayor of New York city this hit was going to be different Benjamín had to go into his office he had not planned how he was going to kill the man just yet. At that point he did not even know where New York was or how he was going to do it. The two cops in the cool one had been tipped off somehow, they were at the scene as Benjamín lands his space ship it did worried Benjamín as such, but the less people know that Benjamin's on the planet the better and easier it was for him to do his job. Benjamin also knows that he has the cops watching him as he lands the vesicle he turns his stealth on nobody can see him on top of the building he sits and waits the cops were thinking where the hit was going to be they believed that it was going to be outside but in fact it was inside that was Benjamin's plan.

The front of the building was guarded who ever tipped them of gave them the wrong information. As the mayor was speaking his last words in his speech he was waiting to receive a bullet, but nothing happened he was guarded but guarded with the wrong information.

Expecting to take a bullet with his bullet proof vest on and all his men what he was told did not happen in a way he was relieved that it did not happen. After a speech which ended we words of something like let's make America a great place and love one another and a load of lovely dove stuff like let's do good to all people, he leaves his testimony with his public. He leaves as he make is way of the stage and down on the concrete floor and back in the large hotel behind him and makes it upstairs s right to the top of the building, there is a helicopter waiting for him.

Benjamin is watching the whole thing he see his future and makes a hit on the mayor he also sees himself escaping he is happy that he sees himself get away. what's to come next was not nice especially if you could visualize it. As the mayor is hassled upstairs Benjamín makes his move he steps out of his craft still in touch with his ship through an ear piece straight to his cockpit to the robot and the space ship they were told to meet him half way. The robot miss calculates as the mayor's team move faster than Benjamín had expected they were moving to the top of the building fast. Benjamin must think and be quick about it.

Although he aware he hits his badge not once but twice giving him the power of invisibility. He raises his arm catching up with the guards just as they reach the top of the building and were entering the big H on the helicopter pad as the helicopter lands Benjamín take is the first shot hitting the guard in the shoulder leaving him on the hard-concrete floor bleeding. When the other guard s turn to return fire there's nobody there they did not have a clue Benjamín fires again taking out a second one, they return fire again but this time it is Benjamín that is on the receiving end of things as he is injured and is hit in the shoulder, but not bad as the bullet that was meant for him hits his badge forcing it to half malfunction as he starts to flicker as Benjamín waits via award with his robot who tells him to wait it was not damaged but will take a minute to reboot Benjamín reply to that is that he has not got a minute and tries to explain that he is on the mayors door step. Benjamin is in luck he manages to take four more guards out skill fully as his suit boots up. The first one takes it in the legs Benjamín walks past him kicking his weapon aside the only reason that Benjamin shot him in the legs was that he did not like killing the innocent. Still injured and in pain he kneels down one knee and send another one down shooting him thrugh the chest one of the guards hides Benjamin was aware as the forth trees to board the helicopter but is thrown off Benjamín was in fixated he did not even notice the helicopter he hits is badge again it malfunctions has in full view of what was left they could now see him, he takes another bullet this time it is in his leg the top of his thigh as he is down on one knee again he take us the chance leaving the mayor and focusing on the helicopter. He looks real hard and sets his sight on the tail then mar arty tips him and tells him to go for the engine he sets himself up a line of fire and then take she shoot missing the first time and blowing the helicopter clean out of the sky on the second. The mayor is on the floor with debris and machine parts in small fire Benjamín slowly walks towards him the mayor is pleading to him.

THE MAYOR:" Wait, we can make a deal."
BENJAMIN: "There is no deal."
The mayor stands s up on his feet Benjamín know that his court means business and do not make deals. The mayor stubbles backward s still pleading.
MAYOR: "look, look."
 That's where it ended Benjamín grabs the mayor pushing backwards until he is on the edge with one more push it was enough to make him slip backwards over the edge of the wall. The mayor had fallen to his death.
Benjamin walks back to his ship just as he is boarding the cops turn up. Benjamin is safe the cops see nothing and Benjamín is off in the cockpit tapping the coordinates of getting his ship back in to space. The two cops are trying to figure out the mess that Benjamín left behind him.
OXYGEN:" What the hell is that."
HITMAN:" I do not know."
OXYGEN:" I do not think the chief will be happy.'
HITMAN:" Get him on the phone."
OXYGEN:" No, but whatever it was it was moving fast. I'm going to call it in."

HITMAN: "This is the cool one to the club we have a UFO Flying over New York can you pick it up copy."
The cops get the reply and the air force is scrambled. Within a few minutes of that phone call Benjamín s robot receive a message that tells Benjamín that his craft had been spotted and now is being followed.
ROBOT:" We are being followed."
BENJAMIN: "followed by what."
ROBOT: "it looks to me to be a fighter jet according to the computer systems there coming in fast."
BENJAMIN: "Try our cloaking devices"
ROBOT: "I have tried there to close."
BENJAMIN:" okay take us up in to the ozone layer the air will be too cold for them to breathe."
ROBOT:" Okay."
The pilot loses Benjamín and his space ship up above the clouds and his theory seemed to work the pilot radios it in
PILOT: "This is voodoo the unidentified object has disappeared I cannot see him anywhere and I have lost him on my radar. I'm coming home."

CHAPTER FIVE
SILHOUETTE

The man that Benjamín is worried about was another assassin called the silhouette he was the only other space being that could have a chance of destroying Benjamín and he could probably destroy the space council. Benjamin knew that they were scared too. They had met on many occasions several infect Benjamín failed to beat him in combat. Also, Benjamin knew that they were rivals. And had to keep looking over his shoulder Benjamín knew how good the silhouette was. Benjamin knew that one day he would look over his shoulder and he would be there. It was the kind of fright that would keep you awake at night.

The silhouette was watching Benjamín very carefully the silhouette had just as many tricks up his sleeve as Benjamín.
The power that he had were like Benjamin's badge infect the silhouette was ten times more powerful which made him ten times harder. The silhouette did not have a spaceship. Even though he resembled a human form he could fly through space pallet to planet without breathing and he could move just as fast as Benjamin's space ship if not probably faster.

The silhouette was at his council the council were discoing Benjamín without his permission and with him not being there. The silhouette was trying to claim that Benjamín was a bad seed and was asking them permission to destroy him. They were going got double cross him as they were slowly begging to believe the silhouette there was a long conversation a head of them the council begin again with a simple question?
COUNTCILOR: "Why are you here."
SILHOUETTE: "To serve you my lords."
COUNTCILOR:" There is a great in balance in your world and you believe that it is Benjamín, am I right."
COUNTCILOR:" is that all you believe."

SILHOUETTE:" If you do not send me to him there will be mass destruction our planets will collide with the human world and planet earth. People will die."
COUNTCILOR:" what powers do you weld."
SILHOUETTE:" I am here to server you all."
COUNTCILOR: "answer the question what powers do you weld."
SILHOUETTE: "Your power."
COUNTCILOR: "Yes your power."
SILHOUETTE: "You do my lords."
COUNTCILOR: "That is all for now on no account are you to approach Benjamín on this occasion."
SILHOUETTE: "Benjamin is a traitor and he deserves to die,"

The silhouette continues.
SILHOUETTE: "Are you blind, is your government so blind they cannot see."
COUNTCILOR: "Hold your tongue, you are dismissed from the council the meeting is over."
The silhouette bows his head and walks out of the court room the councillor's then close the meeting. There is an army of silence as they discuss what they had just heard in the meeting from in the meeting room the council can hear the shouts in anger of the silhouette from inside of the room. The silhouette ws angry over the decision he was smashing things up Ans giving the guards a fight.
COUNCILOR: Do you think he is upset
COUNCILOR: "just a little, however we can just wright Benjamín off he has, or should I say doing his job. There's a lot riding on him and

on the planet earth I believe it is doomed killing Benjamín will not help it, your own child, he is like a son to all of us."
After all the noise the silhouette had finally calmed down the councillors walk out still talking.

CHAPTER SIX
TECHNICAL MALFUNCTION

Benjamin was busy fixing the ship it was one problem to the other as he floats around the room pulling leads out and replacing them, cutting wires and hoping that he was doing the job right, he calls for assistants, but his robot did not hear him meaning that he also had a problem with the robot's communication systems. Benjamin uses a walkie take but the same again he gets no answer.
Second time around he chooses to do it the human way and give us a shout. There's is still no answer. After waiting a few minutes or so he gives up he floats off to find it, the robot is in his cockpit seat, the floe=wars are busy talking which normally meant that something was up, and they normally only talk when Benjamín is around. Other than that, they were mostly silence.
BENJAMIN: "Are you okay mar arty."

There is no answer, as he finds s him he lifts him over on to his back. As he had been working on some of the ships electric she already had the screw driver in his hands he pulls it out of his pocket, Benjamin puts the screw driver into the robot's circuits. There were a few sparks nothing serious but knowing that he might have made a technical malfunction worse.

The robot still does not comply, and Benjamin is at a loss, he might have to return to his home planet and have the robot replaced.

Benjamin has other priority the next target the next hit, as he closes his eyes he can clearly everything he knows that he is close he decides to leave the robots side and think of things by himself. He leaves the robot to fix its self, it was built that way. It was never too late that is what Benjamin was thinking about the next victim. As Benjamin sits in the cockpit he is visualizing the plan of how he was going to introduce himself to his next victim.

Meanwhile the oxygen and the hitman are trying to figure out who is Benjamín and why he is on the planet. And why he is killing people they are left thinking about the two murders. It seems to everybody that Benjamín is not the nice guy who he seemed to be, yet. As Benjamín is above the ozone layer planning the next job, the next move, the next hit, as Benjamín meditates through his mind he sees everything but not just his escape which h leaves him a little confused and not believing it his next victim the profile an actor. The computer up loads his file s and name. Benjamín get the information quickly and wants to move fast. There was something funny about this hit, it did not seem right. In any case he was up for it.

Benjamin was quizzed by the next hit it was a librarian, Benjamín was thinking why? and what? As he had thought that librarians were peaceful people and enjoyed being in silence. Some one upstairs seemed to think deferent, Benjamín did not believe it. Benjamín checks the time obviously he was late. And the assassin must be on time. He callas for his robot mar arty. forgetting that he was out of order and fixing himself at that time he turns to his computer, as he pulls the robot out of the seat and dumps him on the floor next to the sun flowers hoping that he would come around and that the point the sunflowers are singing to bring him back. Luckily the robot had set the coordinates to the planet earth before he had malfunctioned. Benjamin was heading straight for trouble as he zoomed by the robot's coordination he was taking Benjamín away from then planet but that was not want Benjamín wants he has a hit to make and need is to be on the earth the robot was presiding the opposite. It took Benjamin an hour to reperceive with his robot, out he did it by his computer within an hour Benjamín is back up above the earth in the ozone. Hoping that he had not been spotted by British aerospace and knowing that he not being detected. There was nothing on his mind harder. Benjamin wants his old pal the robot mar arty back, two brains are better than one. Benjamin's thinks hard it would be easier as Benjamin now must control the assassination of the third target, while controlling everything in the ship as well as making plans for the target removal. Benjamin thinks it is going to be easy, how wrong he was.

But in fact, it was harder than he thought, it was the opposite Benjamín had followed the librarian by foot straight from his space craft, he was lead to a train station, Benjamin watches in silence. Benjamin realizes that the journey that he was being taking on was too long and he had no time to make an assassination. He was worried that he would be seen making the attempt on that life.

He sends a message to his friend the robot, in the message in a message the message had an address in it. knowing that just recently that the robot had mal functioned and hoping that he had got over it whatever the problem was. Benjamin not forgetting the target and follows him, then the Liberian his journey home was probably his last. Benjamin wants to get close, close enough to lift his wallet. But still there was to many people around the target and him. Benjamin canno0t get a clear shot and the crowds are working on the targets behalf. Benjamin calls to his space ship for assistants, while losing his target for the second time.

The robot is awake and complies to Benjamin's orders. Benjamin gets a good look at the targets face

Benjamin knows that he was close enough to make the hit, if it was only for the crowd being in the way but as he counts it could have been a good thing, but without the right back up things might get a little out of hand. Things might or could go wrong, he was to wait. As he waits for information on the characters identification, it was only a minute before Benjamín had a match. The hair the colour of his eyes and even more so. Benjamin raises his weaponeer. Benjamin believe that he has found the target, he lifts his arm and puts more than a few bullets into the target. Benjamin does not think about it straight away, but he must have put at least half a magazine of bullets into him. What was worrying Benjamin was that it was right in front of the public, that's not good publicity as if I needed it. Benjamin was hoping and thinking that the people were too busy to notice so it was put aside or maybe they were trying to scare as him. It was san orchard situation and even more complicated to explain.

As the librarians was dead and Benjamin was left holding his body as he catches him him just before he hits the floor making sure that he is dead not wanting to but must listen to his last6 requests Benjamín lets him die showing no remorse at all.

The hit was made in a train station and there were many people about and as there was many people around it looks like Benjamín may have got away with it as the people were into minding their own business. Benjamin was able and was clever enough to make the dead target look like dummies leaving him there with a paper on the station bench. As Benjamín waits for a moment to finish him off completely and eliminate his problem he calls for his space ship to come and find him. He calls for his space ship to come and find him, so he can make a getaway.

Benjamin plans on this occasion where to turn to the public he has a problem even though he tried to introduce himself the public were not happy Benjamín in all his angst opened fire killing an old lady who ws throwing herself about, another lady was blaming him for the death of her friend. Another lie. Benjamin's approach to the earth qasr not as welcoming as he would of thought. It sent shockwaves through the entire nation, Benjamín was now all over the news. As Benjamín tried to make it back to his spaceship the crowd was trying to over throw him. His spaceship sat the end of the plat form, as he pushed his way through the commuters and finally escaping he coolly looks at the destruction that he has left behind once aboard the ship the oxygen and his partner the hitman urn up they were not too far behind him.

Benjamin stops before he enters his ship, he stands their just outside the ships bay doors and takes a good look at the carnage that he had made. As he turns as he walks on to the ships deck it is like nothing had happened. He hears a familiar voice the oxygen and then the hitman as they push past the body's that Benjamín had left behind and alive they all had a different story about the hit making it difficult for the two cops to work things out.

Benjamin is thinking that he was lucky to escape, he makes his way back through threw his ship to his cockpit. Benjamin starts a conversation with his robot and computer.

BENAJMIN: "Full thrusters, take me up."

There was no reply but within a minute the computer recognised the order and with a few seconds Benjamín was out of danger and up into the stars. He was back hoovering in and around the ozone, amongst the planets skis.

Benjamin is content knowing that he is safe again as he sits in his chair the two-sun flower sari talking giving Benjamín a lift. Benjamin again falls in to a deep sleep as he is dreaming only a few minutes before he wakes however this are not normal dreams he sees things and hears things he believes that he is dreaming of his or the future.

In the end Benjamin disregards, it was a nightmare and thinks of his home planet he did not know at the time that they were going to double cross him.

Although all the dreams he was having also left a message an exact message and he knew that the silhouette had been watching him there was a positive change in Benjamín s behaviour. As now he knows that he is being watched or followed. Benjamin wakes as the sun rises it looks like it is going to be a long day, Benjamin calls for his robot and looks around for him. The robot was out cold it locks like he had t=run out of energy again Benjamín sails=as he knew that he had been entertain9ng the f=sun flowers. It was too much excitement.

CHAPTER SEVEN
IT IS ALL IN THE WRIST

Benjamin has some time to spare as he is slowly putting his crimes behind him, as he waits for instructions for the next hit. Benjamin needs to find somewhere to practice and learn the skills of the badge. As Benjamín has some time to spare he slowly puts his past of his recent future behind him, as he waits for his next instructions of his next hit. Benjamin needs to find some where he can practice his badge, as Benjamín make sure his arrival to the planet earth is nice and safe, he was looking for some nice land in an area that had not been used. Something derelict or even something hidden out of the way Something on open ground, somewhere he can cloak his ship and not be found.
As he makes his way back to the planet earth he speaks to his computer the computer says to Benjamín that there is no =where and there was nothing on the computer=zed map that would give them the time or space to land. Benjamin orders the ship to land. The computer still denies the ship to land in the end Benjamín tells his computer to find a forest and then continues to ask him if it is a safe place to land his vasal .M array butts in and a whole new discussion begins, in the end Benjamín is right the forest was the right place to Lanes=d Benjamín computer seemed to think differently and the robot had his opinion. Benjamín asks his computer to give him a computerized map of the land that they were in. Benjamín has no choice but to sit in the forest. He lands s his space ship in the trees amongst the forest brown and green.

As Benjamín stands outside of his space ship in the forest, the freshness of the air hits him straight away, this was a lot different from the city, Benjamin wants to change his clothe s as he trees to take off his suit, he struggles as the badge would not let him and he is left as he had started in a suit that he cannot remove. Benjamin finally catches on. As Benjamín plays around with the suit trying to figure it out mar arty finally wakes up and joins Benjamín. Benjamín is outside and has his back to his ship the robot was extending his neck just to watch Benjamín and all the excitement. Benjamin presses his badge not once but three times turning him in to a tiger. The robot congratulated Benjamín. Benjamin calls out to the robot and says I'm going for a stroll. Benjamin was impressed with the badge, as he moved through the forest slowly. Benjamin did not know at that time that he could speak too, his mind was connected to the robot and the spaceships computer as they had started talking.

As Benjamín slowly move s through the forest getting used to be an animal he begins to enjoy the badge as he gets more and More confident he begins to feel it true power and begins to run.
BENJAMIN: "This is awesome I am a tiger."

And he is excited. Benjamin slowly6 gets the feel of the change from man to animal, he is beginning to enjoy the badge. As he is getting more and more comfortable and comp ident he begins to run,

ROBOT:" Your running."
BENJAMIN: "Not yet but I will be."
Benjamin starts to pick up the speed loving every minute of it as he picks up speed he smoothly doges in and out of the forest trees.
As he moves faster and faster, he was a couple of miles away from his space ship, he stops dead right on a small cliff edge. He does not have to use the badge to morph back he merely just has to think it. It takes him a good hour to figure it out. As Benjamín is at the tip of the edge of the small cliff top with the memories of the water fall which is in front of him to take away. Mar arty tells Benjamín where he is and tells him where is going wrong with the badge. He the robot is pupping the knowledge into Benjamín using his mind Benjamín manages to morph back to his half alien half human self. He catches on a within a moment Benjamín back being Benjamin, but only for a moment again he touches his badge and he is off again racing back to his space ship as the tiger. As he nears the destination of the space ship he morphs back to Benjamín he thinks that the badge is increcible and with all the excitement crawls tiredly back on to the ship. With the robot lowering the cargo bays doors as is now on his feet
Benjamin decides that he has had enough of the badge for one day and is eager to speak to the robot about it. As he tries to take his suit off he cannot, forgetting what he had been told that once the badge is on you it cannot be removed. Benjamin is confused but not upset until he gets into his cockpit seat.
The flowers are talking again and joking about Benjamín they laugh with smiles and eventually break into song. The robot awakes Benjamín what was there next destination. Benjamin subjects that they should stay put for now. He still must attempt another trail with the badge. Benjamin was counting that if it was possible for them to stay in the forest it seemed quiet and peaceful. However, Benjamin thinks it might not be such a good idea as there is always someone about. Benjamin does not want the trouble, Benjamín calculates that is two more days before his suit will be ready for the next four tests. After a few days pass Benjamin is ready to make another attempt in the suit he was going to try and morph.

Benjamin stands outside his space ship again by his cargo doors he takes a deep breath the robot has Benjamin's back and extends his next as he watches Benjamín for a better look. Benjamin turns his head a little just getting a clamp of the robot.
BENJAMIN: "Are you ready."
MARARTY: "Ass you are."
Benjamin taps his badge not once, not twice but three times. He disappears for a minute like a hologram. Then he morphs and instead of being one of him there are three of him. Benjamin ask toward she image he knows already that he control them through his mind he vie them a commitment Benjamín again was amazed also because they could talk amounts themselves.

They were a little bit more than a hologram. Benjamin take she lead and tells the first one to reach for his phaser, it does then he tells it put the phaser down on the ground. It does so. Even though the first commandment went okay it was harder to use then the tiger and Benjamín knows that it will take a bit of time understanding this super power. As the day went on day turning into night. Benjamin is giving the last command of the evening which was to get the hologram to pick his reopened up off the floor, mere thought at that point was not working. The next morning Benjamín plays with them all day until he understands s the badges power and it was going to take Benjamín a little more than twenty-four hours to understand the whole badge and not just that the suit too.

Benjamin was concerned for time as he had been there for nearly three days Benjamín was slowly getting used to it, but it was coming slow. Benjamin is believing that there may be a problem a fault in the suit. Benjamin is left to think and find a solution. He comes up with one answer that the badge needs light to work to function at his best or it could be the other way around it needed darkness.

Benjamin continues to study the badge while the darkness that he needs is just coming as the darkness slowly approaches as the sun goes down and disappears over the horizon. Benjamin now can test the badge and suit again.

This time he can feel the power of the forest he could seriously hear the animals of the night. As Benjamin prepares himself to go out into the darkness a full moon and he knew that the wolfs would out on their hunt although it did not darter him.

Benjamin did not want to venture far to the waterfall and back about four miles all in all. As the forest knew him but not knowing its actual powers he had known understood two of the badges powers. As the night went on the calling signs of the wolf packs could clearly be heard. All the other forest animal life seemed to be blocked out due to the wolfs cry. He continues to practice and a was right the suit seems to be powered from and through the darkness. But still worked in the daylight. It was now extremely powerful.

Benjamin was now looking down at his badge and feeling it's power almost straight away it seemed to Benjamín that is was a simple design it was like one of those school badges that you would wear on your blazer except it was like made of mental and it felt weightless. I kind of felt sorry for the person who created it. it ws extremely futuristic either way it was done the badge was on Benjamín

After the evening work Benjamín makes it back to his ship and his feeling tired aware of still being in the forest he closes to sleep outside. He could taste the air it was a little bit better than the city's air. Benjamin find as tree to rest against close but not too far from his space ship.

Benjamin falls asleep under the stars for the first time he does not wake up until the early hours of the morning he is awoken by his robot, it was not normal for the robot to leave his space ship but on this occasion, it was fine by Benjamín. The robot had seen something and wanted to explore he had seen a butterfly and wanted to chase it, the robot was welding g a butterfly net and Benjamín had to smile. He found the robots actions this morning rather amusing. The robot wanted a butterfly to study it was as clear as that the robot did not catch it to his own and Benjamín dismay, but Benjamín had to laugh. Benjamin continues throughout the morning practicing the morphing and finally figures it out save power number two complete. Once this was done Benjamín was feeling a little better. He moves to third, the third power that he welds is the power of defines a shield. As he taps his badge for the third time the badge leaves the suit but only for a second the human eye would not see it but Benjamín could. The badge becomes mechanical and fits into a hole in the lower part of the arm and grow extremely fast reappearing on the top of Benjamín left hand and reshaping It is getting large, large enough to become a shield. The shield is bullet proof Benjamín fins out he thinks that it is amazing. He calls out to his robot to come and have a look he was busy talking to the sunflowers Benjamín calls him again his telling him to bring his phaser. The robot finally walks out down the cargo bay. Once Benjamín had warmed himself up he shouts to the robot to take a few shots at him the robot was quizzed then catches on.

Benjamin asks the robot to stand till as he is experimenting with the power of the shield turning the shield off then on checking how quick it is. He was happy that it worked fast the robot remind s Benjamín that it might even work better in the dark. Benjamin thanks him for his input.
BENJAMIN: "Okay are you ready."
ROBOT: "ready."
BENJAMIN: "Go on fire."
The robot is hesitant as he cannot see the outcome.

BENJAMIN: "Come on take a shot."
Benjamin mind is working quickly unlocking the badge as it goes through its sequences. As the badge move s into his lower left arm he feels the power of it. the shield quickly appears Benjamín with his robot then practice for the =e rest of the day. Until the badge runs out of energy for that one programme. They must wait for the evening to recharge it.

The robot was loving it he would play with Benjamín and the suit for hours teaching Benjamín everything and his ship was just about working too. As Benjamín sits down on the cargo doors he is waiting for the sun to go down and recharge his suit. As the sun was going down it brought a little bit of peace and quiet as Benjamín was just finishing some minor repairs to his cockpit.
BENJAMIN:" I do not know why they have sent us here in this hunk of junk."
Benjamin is trying, and he is working hard as he moves s leads and sockets from his dash board and replaces the components. To fix the ship for a better performance for his next journey. He steps outside and asks his ship to cloak it does and then he uncloaks it. Benjamin is now

feeling a little bit clever as now he can communicate with his space ship through voice. Benjamin is happy but concerned that he cannot wait for the night to come. And he is hesitant about deciding on whether they should leave the forest it might be too soon. Benjamin wants to test the ships speed, but it was to light at that moment and it obvious that he would been scene, and it would be stupid as he would have the authority breathing down his neck. He turns to his robot for a discussion the robot tells Benjamín to hack the air space via the computer and he will tell you wants up there in the skis above.

A few minutes pass and the computer tell Benjamín that there are too many planes up there and it would be dangerous, and they would be in a better position to wait for the night. Benjamin thinks as he tries to find another solution.

Just as Benjamín turns he hears a click there was somebody behind him
BENJAMIN: "Is that you mar arty."
There is no answer and Benjamín is puzzled. He calls out again.
BENJAMIN: "Is that you robot. Stop playing games and get on board."

There's another click even closer than the robot appears he pokes his head just inside the cock pit doors. then he appears to Benjamin's surprise with a visitor.
FARMER: "I have been watching you."
Benjamin knew that what he just said was impossible he would have picked it through his suit and computer. On that account Benjamín knew that he could not be trusted as the man continues.
FARMER:" Did you know that you are a wanted man. You and your space ship are all over the news."
Benjamin knew that it was another lie. Again, his robot would have told him via his computer as the robot once plugged in would have received the broadcast yes, the robot is that advanced he conceive things like messages through his systems that he does not even have to watch.
FARMER: "There is a bounty on your head."
Again, the farmer had told a lie there was no such thing. As the farmer makes himself welcome on the space ship the farmer pushes Benjamín hard enough to knock him into his dash board as the man does Benjamín lands on some button closing the space ship cargo doors the only way in and the only way out. Benjamin has just enough time to press his badge he changes in to the tiger Benjamin takes a swipe at the man knocking the gun that he is holding out of his hands and taking a second swipe knocking the man down as the farmer craws looking for a way out, Benjamín slowly walks towards him pushing his noise and face down upon him Benjamín s says to him that he better leaves before he gets hungry. Benjamin swipes at the farmer leaving him with a scratched face to remember him by. He changed back to Benjamín and opens the cargo doors.
Benjamin continues as the man had only just got on his feet Benjamín continuers that the stretch on his face is for him to remember the day. The farmer gets to run, he goes back into the forest Benjamín find s his weapon and breaks it into tow and throws it into some stubs after he takes the cartridges out he keeps in for a souvenir.

Benjamin did not believe that the man would say anything he was to scare but Benjamín had to make sure and heads straight to his cockpit while he was speaking to his robot thanking him for the backup then shouting at him for letting the man onto his ship.
BENJAMIN: I want all the diagnostics on that man find smutch and pull up his file and file everything that you have just witnessed as from then, when you first met the man.
The robot does as it is told. Benjamin continues with his reaction not sure how he is taken it. he continues to his computer he also tells the computer to check a run on the farmers file. The robots call Benjamín over to him he shows him that the ships cameras on the outside have a recording of it. Benjamín feels an ease.
Benjamin wants a close of the man who claimed he was the bounty hunter Benjamín does not know yet but in the future, he will have one. The robot pulls a picture up on to the cockpit screen.
He is there. Benjamin can now get a better look. Benjamin believes that he will come back probably not on his own. Benjamin cloaks his ship and as he said the farmer came back but this time not ion his own but with a poise. Benjamin was aware of this. Benjamin ship was fully cloaked the only way of them finding it was if they bumped in to it. Benjamín had full view of what was going outside the ship as he was watching via the spaceships cameras. The man was begging to look stupid as the rest of the poise were calling him crazy band other things the man was still content to try and explain. The incident went no farther as the poise gave up and went home. the man's last words where I swear he was hear,
The man was now on his own and Benjamín was thinking of killing him, lucky for the man that Benjamin was level headed and knows by protocol that he cannot just kill any one there had to be another reason and beaming did not have it. so, he lets the man go even though he seen the inside of the ship.

Also, he could only use the badge in self-defence. Benjamin is called the computer the computer tells Benjamín that their game is not over the mean had come back this time with dogs. And they were picking up Benjamín sense Benjamín was slowly bottling himself up.
Benjamin grips his seat with excitement he was one hoping that they would find him. Just one it would take just one of them to bump into the ship and a battle would begin. Not that the human weapons were powerful enough to do any damage they did not know that besides it would give Benjamín something to do. After around fifteen of standing around talking and scuffles this framer was being taken for a fool his friends walk off again. Benjamin knows that he is running out of time and must find another plan=cue to dwell u&ntill his next target. Ads another place to study the rest of the badge. Within a second Benjamin receives a message.
BENJAMIN: "Buckle up were getting out of here."
ROBOT: "Where are we going."
BENJAMIN: "I do not know yet, but my target is at home."

CHAPTER EIGHT
THE TIP OFF

The next target was not going to be easy. This time it was the head of the police force why I asked the question well he was the court man in the city. Benjamin has all his details on file in front of him. Hr=e continues stop read Benjamin tries to laugh this one off Benjamín space craft's position was just below the ozone. He always starts the tasks that he has from there and strategizes his plans. He spends a hole day just watching the targets last moves according to his computer according to his computer he is safety in bed at ten o'clock. Benjamin thinks that time would be perfect to make an approach. Benjamin looked=s again this time he changes his mind he is thinking about half ten that's when he can make maximum carnage the more he thinks the better for him for some strange reason Benjamín watches the video, Benjamín does not know that the film that he is watching was way out of date and probably the wrong film. some body had been sending Benjamín the wrong information and he was just about to check the computer there may had been a fault. Benjamin figured it out almost straight away7, the police chef must have had some brilliant engineers as the information that was brought up onto Benjamín scene was all faze the man that Benjamín was watching was not the man that Benjamín was after he was a look alike quite common in the world of acting. Whoever made this film was extremely bad at it including thee editing.

Benjamin is getting anode as he looks for more information on the real target but there is not any, the police chief certainly knows how to cover his back. There was not a lot of information there anyway Benjamin tells his robot to keep on looking while he goes to look at the other information that his computer had gathered. Benjamin believes that it is a tip off all the information that he usually gets is the right information Benjamín believes that the target now does not even exist and if he does he is existing with a new name. Benjamín take one more look repeatedly and again. Then out of the c=blue the computer finds him taking Benjamín back to the start.

COMPUTER:" He is in."
BENJAMIN:" what is the best time you can give, and I need a destination,"
COMPUTER:" he will be at home exactly ten past ten."
BENJAMIN: "can you pull address and give me a map."
COMPUTER:" yes give me a moment."
Benjamin finally releases the energy and the pressure disappears he has an address and within a few hours the target will be dead.

Oxygen and the hitman heard through the grape vine there was so much information on Benjamín the new bad guy on the seen you could have had a game of chinses whispers. It looked like the farmers had not given in and had told the police about what had happened during the experience of what occurred in the forest yesterday.
The police went straight to the scene, Benjamín crew were lucky, they had left no evidence the ship was built that well. They were looking for clues. However, the farmer was still in shock and his story was not making sense and the police only believed half of the story and the farmer that they were questioning needed a couple of pills to cram his down. The only evidence of t=what the man said was the half-broken gun left in the bushes. The gun went straight to forensics nothing came of it the cops were there for a day or two and could not find a thing even Benjamín tiger paws were covered the badge was quite clever. Oxygen stands there in the middle of the forest ground there was just enough space there was clearly some ground damage on the ground it was oblivious to them but not obvious to anybody else the oxygen could feel it was obvious that something had been there he thinks that the forest had been visited. The oxygen thinks that they have been visited he thinks that the ship was made to be light infect four large mud holes gave Benjamín away. there had defiantly been something have there. The oxygens question was what. The two cops discussed it more, hoping that they would find some more evidence. The oxygen had covered his tracks just in case the space being comes back.

Benjamin had thought that he was safe as he also covered his tracks but his had been found. The oxygen and the hitman knew that the farmer was not lying and had experienced something above the normal. Benjamin was back on the earth.

The two cops baffled and did not know what to do.
OXYGEN:" I want aerospace, I'm going to Have to Make a call I want aerospace to come clean. There are handing something."
HITMAN:" I say tell them to make another move as we are on the ground."
OXYGEN:" that is a good idea, but it will just a matter pf time until we bump into him,"
HITMAN: "he's clever I have to give him that we must have just missed him the tracks that were left behind look reasonable fresh.
OXYGEN:" yeah we know he is up there and we down here, quite clever indeed."
HITMAN:" I want to know his next move."
OXYGEN:" I do not think that it matters."
HITMAN:" how can you say that"
OXYGEN:" I did not mean that last comment it is either that we are extremely bad at our jobs or e are being out classed by an alien.
HITMAN:" okay big boy wants the plan what is our next move I know that he is going to be in our city on planet earth am I right."
OXYGEN: "YES."

HITMAN: "There is a pattern to his killings the link is that they are of the city's most important and wealthy people. What you think that he is doing for the money."
OXYGEN:" No but he is doing it for something or someone. It makes me wonder who is next let's get out of here thus place is scaring me. Benjamin is still up above the clouds looking for information on the chiefs and his where about Benjamín is slowly running out of time. He calls on his robot for some help as he takes one more guess on where the target may be and with a click of a button they are on their way.
MARARTY:" Where is he."
MARARTY:" Benjamín he is at the hotel having a diner party."
BENJAMIIN: "well I have to say that's a fine way to go."
Mar arty smiles.
BENJAMIN: "Set the co-ordinations for the hotel."
His computer does so and then Benjamín finds out that the target can be seen by Benjamín and Benjamín believes he is being set up more and more imagines f=of the target are flooding in through the computer it was alike an art gallery art explosion. Benjamin computer has a lock on the target as the chief walks ion to his room greeting everybody Benjamín knew that he could just walk in, but he wants to wait. He is thinking that he has his target and waits to think of how he was going to do it. he moves towards his weapon cabinet.

He chooses a weapon and one bullet that was all it was going to take. As he was that good he is telling his computer and the robot to stay put not to make contact until they are told. Benjamin awaits in another building across the street e=well-hidden on the roof. It took Benjamín another few minutes to find the target and a just his riffle. As the chief the man that he was going to kill keeps on moving around and with other people around him but once he seated at his table his life was over and another one had just started. Benjamin had him in his sights he slips the bullet into the gun cartridge. And within a few second s had a scope on his target. Within another moment the chief of the police was dead, job done Benjamín calls apron his shipman the people in the room look around dazed and confused. The shot could not be heard as foe the make of the riffle. It had a silencer the only sound was the sound of the glass cracking as the bullet went into the body. With the building being in a narrow street nothing the echoes of his people shouting in amazement could be heard.

As Benjamín calls for his Robot and asks him to make an approach to him as he is in the clear. The space ship was nearby, and Benjamin was picked up in a jiffy as be boards the ship he speaks to himself. As he gets a good look of what is left of the chief which was not a lot. Benjamin was pleased three down four to go.

Benjamin now must make an escape his turns up uncloaked, funny enough this time the escape was easy there was nobody around and all the people were down stairs in and on the streets. Although screaming and shouting could be heard. Benjamin boards his ship, he can feel the sorrow he has in side of him and around his soul. This was a knew feeling and thinks that he may have killed the wrong man. Benjamin is standing as he puts his phaser down. He looks at his computer and tells it the coordination's and tells him to take him there. Benjamin needs time to cool off there was nothing like above the clouds. Not forgetting that the man that he had just killed. He closes his eyes and falls to sleep.

The robot takes to the cockpit and gains control of the ship and the two sun flowers are talking amounts themselves both keeping an eye on things and keeping the robot company.

It was a few days until Benjamín had awoke the flowers had done their job. That was watching over him, and the planet earth. Benjami9n is still stuck in his space suit he continues that he was finding it hard to move around joking to the flowers who could see clearly that he was having a little trouble moving around.

Benjamin tells his robot to move over as Benjamín wants to take a seat. They were both sharing the chair. Looking down straight at the

planet earth Benjamín starts a discussion about how long it was going to be there. With all the facts coming out, the robot compliments Benjamín as his knowledge was as good as his. His knowledge was in fact perfect. They continued to discuss it through out of the day until his robot asked him to stop. As the robot said this is over load started meaning that he needed to charge himself up after a few sparks Benjamin knew that he was serious and not bowing out of the conversation because he had been beaten for knowledge.
Benjamin laughs the robot tells him that it is no joke. The planet earth was serious business it was there business now.

Benjamin replies to the robots last words are the humans really that bad. Are they really destined for their own destruction?
The robot answers with you said destruction. They start a new conversation and had started talking about the wars of the planets past. They were both hitting each other with perfect reply's and beating

each other disagreements with correct answers. It had become a verbal argument from a serious but friendly conversation. Benjamin new what had happened the robot was just expressing itself and its compo ants as Benjamín did his mind. They both finally conclude that the planet was doomed because the humans did not care for it enough.

CHAPTER NINE
IN DEEP WATER

    Benjamin was board of being in OutSpace or there about even more so being up in the earth's ozone. He wants to go back down to the earth he was thinking under the sea the ocean. He already knew that there was a possible chance of the ship being found by the submarines, but he was going to take a chance he tells the robot that heat might be fun being chased again by a couple of submarines. He taps in the coordinates and makes a quick departure from space to the ocean water. His space ship was also built to move underwater, he finds somewhere to rest his ship it was a nice sand bank at the bottom of the ocean. He had taken the ship right down to the bottom of the sea. Benjamin begins to settle as he is watching the wild life and is finally relaxed. It ws one of his favourite places on the earth or should I say under it.

Benjamin enjoys the views he seems to be with one with himself and everything that surrounds him. The robot wants to join in and is getting excited and the flowers Aare chanting it seemed to Benjamin that it was a good idea after all as everybody was happy. As they all watch the sea life.as the time went by the smaller fish in the sea were departing and the larger sea life were coming out to play.

Within a few minutes Benjamín ship is surrounded by sharks they know that Benjamin is there, and they were swimming closer and closer Benjamín is fascinated and closes his eyes. Some of the shark's bump on the ship Benjamín believes that it is a warning just to let Benjamin know that they are there. Benjamin is cool about it as he leans over to a small fridge he opens it and pulls a can of beer out of the fridge door side still half watching the sharks.

As he puts his feet up on top of his dashboard he opens the can of v=beer. The sharks were now getting more and more violet they defiantly knew that there were some kinds of presents there. Benjamin still was just happy to sit there.

Although the robot was not to keen and looked as little bit worried. As much as the robot liked the sea life in the day time in the night time it made him feel uneasy under the water he was all over the place and would not stop saying more oxygen I cannot breathe and on top of that sharks.

Benjamin although humoured takes control of the situation and turns his robot off, it was nice and quiet again. As the sea life slowly depart Benjamín is left with the full view of the sandy floor. And the full view of the ocean above.

Benjamin had not ever had the chance to experience being under the ocean before or had not had the opponent to swim in the sea. He had begun dreaming maybe that's why he was drawn to this place under the ocean waters.

As Benjamín sits and continues to watch there are all kinds of life emerging around him as he watches from the inside of his ship. He had not yet learnt the names of the species that are entertaining him. He wanted to know all the names of these new creatures he watches in extrapolation. And falls fond of it. it was even more angering as he was falling in love with being amount them. he wanted to know if they could communicate with them. As he has puzzled himself with his own thought over them.

Benjamin closes his eyes and falls asleep with the new thought he dreams of being on his home planet the robot wants to surface he ws scared of that type of wild life Benjamín tells it to put the thought in to his mind as the robot was just about to decide Benjamín give s in and tell the robot to take the ship up and back up above the earth. The robot takes the ship up of the ocean floor and surfaces junta foot above the ocean waves. The robot feels a lot better Benjamín was in a sulk as he was enjoying himself. Benjamin knows that there is going to be trouble Benjamín and his crew stay put.

In the meantime, Oxygen and the hitman a few days later turn up at Benjamín last items scene any gain they find nothing it was the same except before they time to get there the police had cleared the scene. Everything had to go conferences and ballistics they needed to know what kind of bullet it was when they got there the bullet shell matched the one that came out of the body of the item and fitted the now empty cartage although there is no match for the bullet it defiantly did not come from the earth. Oxygen and the hitman were surprised, they knew that they were on the right tracks. They were both thinking the same.
OXYGEN: "It sure looks like our little play mate has a thrust for blood."
It was obvious that the bullet was from an alien weaned and the Oxygen and the Hitman discuss every detail. They were still on the roof where the shot was taken. They were talking about how much security that the target had and weather it ws adequate. The Oxygen

believing that he was poorly guarded either that or the man who shot was an extreme special shot. The hitman continues he believe s that it was the same man and now they were looking for a serial killer. Oxygen agrees and could see where the conversation was going. Oxygen could not make himself any clearer, looking at the evidence.

CHAPTER TEN
CODE

Benjamin needed a code to get inside their systems, but the code was not with me or in my mind I had not got the message that I was being followed by an Assassin and I was an assassin. There was going to be lightning and thunder I could feel the wither changing in my sleep. as I laid in my capsule fast asleep I was dreaming of my next target it was to be a shop assistant. I had taken in consideration that this target was going to be easy. I had not taking inconsideration of this target as he was a young man and going to be a dead one by the computer. I closed my eyes and fell back asleep looking for more information on him hoping that the dream would bring it and tell me the rest. I was in my chair and not in my bunk not that it made any difference. The images of the things that this young man had done were piling up I could see everything clearly. It ws like watching a film of myself everything that I had ever done everything that I had ever seen. Since that I had approached the planet earth. I was just waking up with the knowledge that I had received in my sleep. I cannot explain it right now, but it was extremely interesting. As I woke up in a cold sweat. I was drenched I did not know whether it came from my mouth or my mind as I awoke I floated through the space ship thinking about the next kill. Meantime the two cops down on the earth were thinking of my last kill I believe that there was no evidence as I had cleaned it all away they could never blame me as the bullet that I used came from my planet and did not exist on the earth.

They thought that they were clever, but I was trice as educated as them. I floated around towards my computer. The robot had recorded everything, this is where it hurt the memories, the remorse, and the thought of killing them. I now knew that I had missed the target somehow, I, are the mistake as I took his soul into my body I had realised that I had killed the wrong man.

I was chilled even though I had missed the target and I was still cool even though I could feel some anger for stupidity I knew that I was good enough to make another attempt.

I wanted to go back to the woods, but I feared that I would raise suspicion all over again and I knew that it would be trouble.

There was a bounty on my head this time it was a real one. I guess that I could always go back to the bottom of the sea. It might be safer down there than up here, a part of the submarines. I could decide given a bit of time as, so I decided to stay amongst the clouds or just above them. The flowers were teasing me over what had happened the robot did not make a sound even though he wanted to say something I could tell by the look on his face. I told them all to shut up even though none of them were speaking.

I had to make a report, so I just got on with it. I was beginning to think that thing s were going to go wrong and that scared me.

Even though I had faith some people might think I was short of it. At that point I closed my eyes it was all I could do. I fell asleep knowing that I would find the answer and peace.

The dream that in was having of the third victim to me seemed pointless it was of the normal boy a human Benjamin can see no wrong in him and had only a few hours before had all the information on his entire life little it may be short. It was insignificant to the plan. Benjamin tells his computer that he is confused. It was now too late to go back home to get the real facts it was just to late. Benjamin closed his eyes this time leaving his mind his semi consciousness it was rally that he would do that in his sleep, but he did not that he could sleep in fact he had not slept at no point when he was on the earth. It seemed to him that the planet was really doomed he wanted to know something that was where the plans that his planet were having were they about saving the planets future., either way I reminded myself that humans had sold itself out. And it was my job to make sure that the deal is done.

Benjamin was on the planet following the boy along. His movements were as usual pretty much the same. I had been following him for a couple of weeks it still did not make any sense. The next hit was rattling Benjamín s brains he turns to the computer and got nothing he turned to his robot who finds the solution. That the boy was put there to confuse the situation Benjamín quickly understood and was happy that he had an excuse, so he did not have to take the young boys life. Benjamin knows now that he is being set up. Benjamin takes to the cockpit and takes his ship up in to space into a place that he felt safe. He was nice and relaxed and waiting he was still thinking about the boy he ws thinking that he would let him go. He knows that it was a mistake to take the council and make decisions on them behave but on this occasion, he did just that, he was beginning to think that he was losing his mind. Any other time he would have just done the job in hand. In the end Benjamin bows down to his council he could feel the power of all of them thinking for him he knows that he must kill the boy target he loads up his phaser steps out of the space craft he knows all the boys moves and waits until he in front of him. He wanted the boy to him as boy just stands innocently Benjamín raises his arm the boys raise his arms and then speaks asking him if he was under rest no Benjamín continues your dead. But something was wrong it was not in my nature to kill the innocent I'm sure that somewhere down the line there was a mistake the boy knew I could not do it and I knew that I could not do it vi had been sent the wrong target again.

Benjamin believes now that he was being set up to fail and was on his way back to his home planet what impressed him the most that the boy was willing to take the bullet. Once I was back on the space ship plugged in the coordinates and buckled everybody in, I was doing this fast as that is the way I moved.

Benjamin wanted to speak to his council about his next kill the next victim I could see that they had done know wrong. the kind of thought that Benjamín was having were of trees and murder the council was there straight away and as they all appeared I started to put my complaint forwards.

After a long meeting they finally agreed that they might have wrongly entered his systems believing that his was somebody else they also agreed that the killing were just, and they said that I let the boy go. Benjamin was pleased not knowing approaching the council was a mistake as in the future the council's truth would come out it ws a big mistake by him and a bigger mistake by the commanders however Benjamín had convinced them for now.

The councillors last words were before the meeting ended were we have given the boy a chance, but it means nothing

I put aside as I had better business to do it was not nearby as I could have been doing other things. I went for the next target not forgetting the chief of the police which I also got a grilling for by the council. The next target was a prisoner I had to get this one right or that would be the end for me as it was also just spoken about in the council rooms. I could not afford to make any more mistakes. This guy the prisoner he was basically running the city's underworld from his prison cell. Everything that moved in and everything that moved out this guy was a real scum bag he was a daddy the big daddy. I changed the coordinates and moved the space ship. It was time to use the suit again as checked if the suit was fully charged and keeping one eye on the time I had all his details running through my mind everything my escape then NY approach and how many guard s were there and even what his reaction would be before I got there.

I was getting closer I could feel his sickness I was nervous that was the first time that I felt worried it was not like me. in could make the hit that is all my mins =d would let me say. As I morphed myself in to invisibility it seemed like I could just walk in, but it was walking out which was going to be the problem. It was in their ground s that I had found the game had begun it did not take belong to find him, but he had so many covers it was hard to get to him. I had failed again my superior were not happy they could see that I could see that.

Benjamin had told his guardians his saviours that he could not make the hit there were to many doors and people about he reacted fiercely to what Benjamín had said they were unhappy and were discussing whether Benjamín could do his job. Even more so weather or not he was good end ought to do his job. I was being pulled aside as Benjamín had lost his temper. There were many answers to why Benjamín did not full fil his missions. They were many questions which were going unanswered as Benjamín did not know the answers to the questions that were being thrown at him. He loses his temper again. In the end the council gave Benjamín a bit of le way. They gave him the chance to do his job again their words were do not fail us. Benjamin told them that he needs time to think, they agree. He leaves the court room and goes to his room when he gets there the robot is there to greet him Benjamín is tired and pushes the robots welcoming, Benjamin lie down on his bed. Then greets the robot. He was happy that the boy had be granted amnesty it makes it better for Benjamin one less person to kill. As he dreams he see everything knowing that he must go way back into the past to see where he went wrong and if he can catch up with the two corrupt targets as he dreams he hears the word s you have been sucking up and he was a squalor a big mouth. With no control verbally or mentally. He woke up in the end while dreaming of putting a bullet in some guys head it was a nightmare. In the dream it retook Benjamin a day and a =n evening to find him as I awoke I was still on the planet but in my room. Benjamin grabbed mar arty and headed to my space craft the bullet that he was dreaming about was for him he was making a quick escape.

I made my way back to the space ship something was not right it seemed to me that I had a hit on a target which had a hit on me which I should not have hit. I knew that I was going to have nightmares over this one. However, if name was on the list then his name his on the list. As the boy did not fit in I think that I found the real target I left the body on the road where it could be found. Within a few hours the cops both were on the scene. Oxygen is taking a close look while the hitman locks around thinking if this was Benjamin. As Benjamin thinks that he ships was cloaked the two cops get a glimpse of something that they think is not there Benjamin is watching clearly and realizes that his cloak is off as he switches it on the two cops draw their weapons.
OXYGEN: "Did you see that."
THE HITMAN: "yeah I did."
OXYGEN:"
Oxygen and Hitman raise their arms believing that they had found the target Benjamin meanwhile as they approach the ship is turning everything off telling the computer to shut everything down as he recloaks his ship and takes it ten feet up into the air. They did not fully approach Benjamin, but they knew that his presents were there I believed that they saw the shape of the ship and that's all.

After the close encounter he decided that I should go home back to my planet and council at that time I did not know that I could only approach the planet if I was invited. As I walked in to the great halls un invited the councillors began to question right there I was trying to tell them about the experience back on the planet earth.
The council began to question me first telling me that I was wrong to approach them at this time the conversation went on for hours all over the target that I had missed I began to complain, telling again over and over that the computer was in control at that time and it was not his

mistake but their s and the computers. I had just enough evidenced to convince them that I was only trying to do my job. The sentence for this was doing time this time I had lost. I thought that this was a little harsh I knew the planet that they would be sending me too. The conversation went on and on the council, were being extremely hard it was still unknown to them that the silhouette was still breathing down my neck. Up to the point that I stared a fight with h_m as I pushed him to the floor then telling him to get up. As he I floored him again it took everything in my powers to try and convince them that my words were true, and I was stalling the truth. At this point the council decided to re-evaluate and kindly asked me to start again a new interview. This was going to be the hardest thing of my life and the evidence was against me. I as wit coming the silhouette was just getting off the floor as he raised his sword as he was now behind me and was about to attack me, as the council laid witness to it the guarcs that were supposed to protect me did not they just stood there. The first time he missed yelling that he had had enough the second end time I was on the floor with his sword against my chest he movec backward s removing the sowed from me. and started all again I was looking for my sword, but I did not have one according to the councillor know weapons are allowed in the court room I was lucky as they could clearly see that it was not me that was braking their laws. I could feel it he ws hoping that I would use the badge he was trying to set me up. I wanted to show the council that it was me that was full of goodness but, yet I was still the betrayer. The silhouette drops his sword realizing where he was and kneels on the floor even though with a bad temper he ws still calm. I knew that I could not continue with his personal battle as I was unarmed. As he had got up on his feet and was now slowly moving around me in a circle he talking to me it like he was putting curse upon me. I could feel every word as he walked behind me again this time calling me a liar he raises his sword for the third time as he was about to stake me down. The guards move in, the guards grab hold of him but not begore he strikes one down, He falls to his knees still talking to the council his words were let me kill him as the silhouette shouts he is dragged out of the great hall. After the events in the court room Benjamin is given amnesty and he was free to go. But not before he bows down to the silhouette as I walked towards him knowing now dangerous he was Benjamin greeted him polity and bowed my head.

Benjamin ws hesitant but happy that he can now go on his way. When I had got home I tapped my security code into the door lock, but it did not open, I tried again I was confused. As I tried again then again, I got the same answer as I turned around I bumped straight in to some guards three of them in fact I was thinking at that time that I was at the wrong address. The had me in a corner they were not being particularly nice as they shave dame around a little, the fist guard tapped me on the back I had turned my back to them to give me time to think. It did not work, I was s being set up again as the guard continued to prod me I knew not to turn around but to answer them. and that is all I can remember about that encounter as hard as I was theatre was no way that I could beat them without the space to change. When I awoke I was on a totally different planet I had been kidnapped I awoke in chains in a cell the bed was broken, and its pillow was on the other side of the room. There was a basin and a toilet on the side of the cell in its corner. I wanted to call out, but I could not speak it felt like I was on something I had been poisoned. At that point I was thinking that I was losing the gift to communicate. I could feel my eyes it looked like I took a bit of a beating on top of things. As I tried to call out there was nothing I was trying to think where I was if I could find my new destination I could send a message to my robot and computer to hail them. As I waited for my voice to return I could clearly see that there was a jug of water on the side, I ws beaten I just wanted to kick something it would have been better if my hand sewer untied I would be able to pick it up.

As I sat down with no food or heat every day for the next few years was a nightmare in the end I was now beginning to break no food nothing a cup of water at the very least. I was smashing rocks day in and day out still did not speak to anybody even that my voice had grown back. I was into keeping myself to myself. And when was approached I told the person to leave me I ws not in the business of making friend I was an assassin. I was breaking rocks and the food

everyday was getting worse and worse not that I would eat any of it as I was supplied with everything through my suit.
The food was basically a hand full of vegetables and a cup of water I called it my brothers laugh sane was giving my portion to the guy that I was chained to but only when I was working on the grounds. As many times that he had thanked me I still did not speak to him.
The cells were cold and with no light and the darkness was the only place that I wanted to dwell.
After the beating s and the whippings, I was beginning to give in I ws looking at the stars calculating the exact time by the stars it was coming up to my fourth year of prison. My space ship still had not turned up. Every so often the guards would come in to the cell and try and remove the suit from me. I cannot count how many time s they had tried it was just a matter of time before my robot would find a way of finding me I was pledging all my confidents in him.
It was no use at this moment a few past I was truly screwed I could hear my consciousness telling me everything that was going to happen to me I was still in touch but only just meanwhile back on in the councillor's room they believed that I had one a runner and was handing on the planet earth they sent their assassirs the silhouette too finds me when he told them he could find me he was punished also.

A cargo ship came by every two weeks leaving more prisoners and it ws heavily guarded the shackles that I was wearing did not leave me room to maunder as for the guy that was chained to did not make the planed escape any easier. Every time the ship came I just bowed and the thought of sorrow that I was left there on the concrete. I must have dug a thousand metres in the planets soil. The thought of it was not helping it was become at that point adductive in the end I felt I could not work on longer I weak and tried and starved there was nothing left of me. I had fallen on to my knees, I had become a slave that was far from being the super human that I was before I was brought here. The suit was not working either the prison girds had smashed it so hard with me in. as I was just about to give up I could see something approaching the court yard they looked like the guards back in the councillors Greta halls as the ship lined the guard s walked out. The guards were ordering everybody to lie down as I was about to lay on the floor one of the guards stooped me and he spoke his words where you are free come with us. I raised up my shackles he pointed his weaned down on the ground ignoring the man that I was attached to and within a second my feet were freed. the pensioner swore cheering as he realises the shackles around Benjamin's wrists. They march him away. Benjamin could not believe it he was free and extremely happy.my space ship had landed I felt sorry for some of those people aa lot of them were innocent, I viewed to that day that I would come back with justice.

After I had been taken back to my quarters after the councillors had interviewed me I was taken away to be cleaned up after I had renewed my suit and was greeted by the robot and the sunflower s I was asked to stay around until I was fully nourished in my new suit after a while may be a few days my normal way of thinking came back, and I was thinking about who set me up. I was on my way back to the planet earth to finish the job.

My robot brought me my new suit I was happy to take it as I was shaving the long grey beard off I ws talking to the robot. I ws telling him that I had not ever felt that weak. Anand as weak as I was I cleaned my sleeve up again. As I walked out of the bath room I could see that the robot had brought my two sun flowers to great me and they were happy and as entertaining as always.
I changed my clothes and was back in the suit again. The robot did not want to tell me as he thought that it would hurt Benjamin, but he could not lie and told Benjamin that it was the silhouette that had set him up. Benjamin told the robot that he knew that already. And told him not to mention his right now we will talk bout it another time and I will approach the council when I am called. The robot agrees. As Benjamin had closed his eyes he was sending his mind not in one the future but back to it, he sees that there had been a great argument and the silhouette had destroyed the council and made another one by his name. as Benjamin wore the suit he had the right to approach him but only if invited he could see that happening soon. Benjamin wants to get out of the planet quickly, Benjamin was going to depart back to the earth but first he takes a glimpse of his future.

The robot went off on one as Benjamin and its self were boarding the space ship Benjamin jumps in the cockpit as he is setting the ship up for take-off the robot is still talking about the planet and they are having the conversation as Benjamin taps the coordinates the planet earth. He knows already that he was going to be followed that was the last of Benjamin worry's as he must save his own planet at the same time.
A new council had been made Benjamin could understand why. A new council was about them and they were brought more peace as Benjamin raises his ship up to take off. he could feel that the people were not happy as much as Benjamin wanted to stay around he had a job on the planet earth. Benjamin new that there was going to be rioting. It was out of his hands at this moment. As much as he wanted too to stay he was explaining to the robot he had to leave this played

on Benjamin's consciousness for a while as he taps in the coordinates to the earth. The robot had so many questions that it would twist your mind. He continued they said that they wanted peace, yet they were killing their innocent their very own peace keepers for speaking of peace.

I ws thinking that the planet ws not governed enough and soon it will destroyed and there was nothing that we would be able to do but turn to the planet earth. It was not in our nature, but I had to close n=my eyes again asking myself questions after questions why was I thinking the worst.
It was not my job to do the thinking, it was my job to kill. I closed my eyes yet again for another time I was counting on the thought to leave. If the council knew what I was thinking they would have me in the council room again a d judged.

As I made my way back into space as I approached the earths solar system I was heading straight for the planet it was night time as I waited for the night time after the second morning I was back in the wood s testing out the new suit this time it came with head gear I was hoping that I would not disturb any thing I did not want the farmers coming after me again. I already knew the powers of the suit I could morph in to a tiger I could also have invisibility and I could weld a shield. I ws now thinking and getting g more excited I was going to tap the badge for a fourth time to see what would happen as I did after wasting all the energy on the frill of the badge there ws nothing I was impressed but confused I restate badge with my mind and tried again and again nothing. I was doing something wrong. I called the robot outside.

With my robot by my side I did it again the same thing happened again for some strange reason the robot was refused to help me he said that on this one Benjamin had to figure it out for himself. After an hour I had to give up it was getting dark Benjamin steps absurd the ship and cloaks it. temerity is waiting. And asks Benjamin if he had any luck on that point the robot and Benjamin sit down and discuss the history of the badge where it came from who knows its true power and everything else and especially how it was found, there was an extremely long story to the badge and its makers.

According to the story the third part of the badge needs to hear the wearers voice and the word is that are to be spoken are the word and number S P I R I T 5. Benjamin is excited as now that he has the robots word he can continue with the study of the badge. Except it is dark the right place to tune and re energise his suit but the wrong time to play with it.
Benjamin was willing to give it another go but he would have to wait until sun rise believing in badge and its words.
Again, nothing had happened the robot tells him to say it with politely and say it like you mean it as I did the third power was their like it came out of nowhere, but Benjamin still could not figure it out. h knew what the robot was going to say figure it out for yourself. Benjamin was frustrated knowing that the robot had the answer and would not tell him.

Benjamin is delighted by the power od=f the badge even though he cannot find the fourth power he as the morning come he is outside trying to figure it out and not having much luck. He starts with under tapping the badge and keeps commanding its shelled the idea qasr simple enough, Benjamin just needed a bit more time. As he sits there weighing up the odds that that within a couple of days tab police will back. In the meantime, he would stay put in the forest and try and figure out the next super power of the suit. Benjamin just thought that he should look around the forest as it seemed to him to be a nice and quiet place and the wither was holding as he walks he keeps on getting the urge to run in the end he gives in and breaks out in to a sprit he had found the fourth power of the badge stealth. As he moves faster and faster unseen he was feeling good as he makes it back to his space ship he is happy to tell the robot who in return congratulates him. Benjamin is happy.

Benjamin sits down in his bunk he is tried as much as the day, the gift that he received that morning made him feel. As the night comes quickly he thinks of the next and last super power as he has now super speed stealth. He was feeling excellent and wants to practice more he was becoming more and more confident. Benjamin wants to go outside the robot warns not to over indulged and now is worried Benjamin ignore s the robot's advice and heads outside any way a little unusual fir Benjamin the robot tells him to be careful Benjamin reptile what's the worst that could happen. As Benjamin practices the skills of the badge through the night he getting better and better as he get used to it and good at it he spend sell day clicking g and unclicking his badge until he tired he walks back to his space ship completely exhausted all he wants to do is lie down he is tried again before he gets the chance to settle down the robot is there talking to him telling him that the bounty hunters and the famer were back, became knows why he has left his ship uncloaked as he thought it would be safe handing in the darkness of the forest.

There are no weapons on the ship as it is a ship of peace Benjamin stand sin full view if the bounty hunters he is feeling tired and die snot know if he has the energy to full fill the battle which was ahead. The crowed of people are shouting at him he is feeling more and more for the fight as Benjamin is being told not to harm any of them and must think of a way of other's approaching them or getting back into his space ship and fin ding another destination. Benjamin could see clearly that he was going to be in the morning papers again.
FARMER:" I told you, I told you that he ws their but none of you believed it."

Benjamin was going to try Ans reason with them now that's all he could do.

The robot just tells him to make something up. Benjamin's reply to that was what I am standing here in front of a mob.

The robot tells Benjamin to tell them that he is an experiment from American aerospace.

Benjamin does not think that it would work but he tried it. with a little bit of work to the that last comment things were looking a little bit quieter the robot was telling him to play along Benjamin had never had the chance to act he was getting into the role quickly.

As more and more questions were put to him he finally told the that he was smeary here to protect the environment and that it. he continues that the space was all part of the programme to scare the Germans.

They finally agree, and they leave Benjamin alone again. Benjamin walked d back on to his ship bursting into laughter that was hilarious your clever little robot I have never had so much fun. The crowed disperse and the farmer gets it in the neck again.

BENJAMIN: "You could have given them a chance at least one."
MARATRTY: "It is my job to protect you. Tat what I did now get on the space ship please."
Benjamin does as he is told and gets on the space ship. He continues the conversation the returns answers for his actions the robot even though Benjamin had not opened fire and killed the group of men he

knew that it was protocol and he was now getting a grilling like what it would come out when he gets his summoning to the council.
After the long conversation with the robot as tired as Benjamin was they both shut themselves down the robot plugs its self in for a recharge and Benjamin lays out on his bed, the sun flowers are singing him to sleep. this time there's no dreams just crying as Benjamin's upset over the last days out goings as he trees to tune ate radio and in the end, get fed up throwing it across the room only for gravity to put it back into his hands. As he plays around with it as he pushes it away leaves it floating around the ship. Benjamin finally settles down Benjamin is worried, as he must dream of the silhouette he knows that he is close to him but only in his mind. The silhouette was not the man you would want in your mind the thought of thinking of him could destroy you. Either way I was going to put up a fight.

CHAPTER ELEVEN
BROKEN CIRCUTS

Ass I thought about who set me up and gave me a good five years I ws concluding that it was the silhouette the though sent ne back five years thinking that I as lucky, but the pain still existed. Every thought every fear of what could have happened and what happened. Back then I knew that it ws name it was not knowing s to me I could see clearly, I just wanted my revenge. I thought about him more and more as until I believed that I was now in his mind rather than him being in mine. I was trying to thin k about other things the d=good thing and the dad things it was not easy, but I was getting it right for now. I did not think that the silhouette knew that I knew, and we were both playing the game the thoughts of him were taking me to the edge and likewise I was driving him crazy. He wanted my badge, I could not give it to him you see it was awarded to me and once the badge was on it could not be removed, valour by the council unless he was up there making new rule is the badge stays on. He had none, I knew that if we were e to come to battle I would win. He did not k now that I was playing the same game as him from now. I put myself into his mind this time with the badge as my guidance, as my weaponeer, I might have a chance to destroy him and that was all to come.

Thinking about him was given me a trill. Thinking what was going to happen in the future ws giving Benjamin a cold sweat and enough thought's. Benjamin tyres to think and he goes over it like a script repeatedly until he finds the answer and is happy again. It was finally sinking in, but it would eventually pass. As I had business son the planet earth. Her was salt to think about the destruction of my home planet had happened that was what the robot was trying to tell me it happened while I was in orison and the destruction of our seven guests which was opt he earths planets hope.

If the silhouette gains power, he will destroy everything I was not going to let that happen. I was concerned for the planet who would not be. as I spoke to the robot letting him know that I knew that my family were dead through the court by the silhouette and his destructive behaviour.

I had enough of sorrow and I was on my way back to earth I knew who the target was it ws the boy gain again I was trying to resist and I knew

this time that the council controlling=g the killing was not to be messed around with I had no choice be=vein though I has=d feeling =s to the job. I did not have time to gain the ken obliged to make it look sweet I just had to kill him as he left his shop as us I was there it was straight forward I pulled my gun and took a good look at him within the next couple second she was dead two bullets threw the chest, he knew and I knew it was his time after I had killed him I looked at the body but only for a minute as I walked away it was time to give the police a call. I was thinking how I was going to use the suit.
Something had gone wrong I was projected in to the future and I was at the next hit the next target I knew where ea. was but I did not know why it had happened after the hit of the boy the power of the thought had sent me way into y=the future I did not have to do thing I was right infant of my target as I sat in the middle of the room because e in a corner would be to obovoid I hid behind a paper the___14 old fashioned d way to spy I saw the target but before I had a chance to eliminate him form the list something strange happened again I was back looking at the body of the boy. when I got back to my ship to explain to the robot what I had just experienced thaw robot could not find answer as he was not present it looked like Benjamin had to figure it out for himself.

As I walked back to the space ship I was feeling anger over what I had just killed even though the thought in the café was a calming one the force of killing somebody so young ws hurting me. my space ship had arrived, and I walked on up into the cargo bay and on to the ship.

BENJAMIN:" What's going on."

ROBOT:" It Seems to me that there is pattern to are killing this has to be= changed."

BENJAMIN:" it does not make a difference the outcome Is the same."

ROBOT: "I know it is just harder. I do not know the answer all I know is that the chief was supposed to be next."

BENJAMIN:" That does not make it any easier.

As the whole thing went through my mind feeling like my old self again. As I went to find some where to calm down I found a café it was extremely busy, and I looked out of place through this I could not get served at the counter I place d myself down at one of the tables a few minutes later as a waiter came to me I asked for as black coffee and she took the order within a few more minute I was feeling better. I was looking at the menu I walked out forgetting the order and left the café the waiter was not too far behind me and I told her to forget it as I had to be somewhere. She looked up set and I was just as confused, As for the expression on the face.

BENJAMIN:" It cannot make any=difference a hit is a hit am I right I cannot go home because it is no longer there. What is the answer, answer me?"

Benjamin for the first time loses his r=temper, the robot is confused to see hemin that state Benjamin tells the computer to turn all the systems off and asks his robot to help him to his bunk he knew exactly what it was the new suit was setting in. knowing that now he must find and climate with no excuses the targets as he thinks of this in his sleep he also knows that he is in danger. He knows that he was to blame and if he did blame somebody it would be the computer even more so himself. He tells the computer to take him back into the past he has the victims address he taps in the coordinates and makes his way there while Benjamin talks to his computer it explains why he ws miss guided and why he got the target wrong the first time. This time it was the chief. Benjamin steps outside of the dark shadows of the street the road swore half lit as he watches the chief from up=underneath a large tree. The chief is making his way up his garden path Benjamin believes that it was the right time to make the kill. As the chief unlocks the door Benjamin a=can to catch up with him as the chief unlocks the door he walks in side closing the door as Benjamin just gets there it ws right tp0 the point of being in his face. the chief turns on the living room lights and pours himself a drink.

The cop knows that he has got company and makes it easy for Benjamin to film=ND him. The chief is no coward he was a killer and he was fed up with the game he was fed up with his life. Benjamin walks in techier has his back to him. As he puts down the tumbler glass on to the table which was near to him. He continues to talk to Benjamin, Benjamin could see exactly what he was doing he was trying to talk himself out of it. Benjamin tells him that he is no god and if he was looking for him he would better look hard. Benjamin tells him that he is there to kill him. Benjamin does not mess around the chief turns around again showing him Benjamin's back as turns around again Benjamin gets a good look at him, making sure this time it was the right person the right target. It was not a fake dressed up in a police uniform. Benjamin takes a step forwards and raises his arm. A few minutes later Benjamin walks out of the house the chief was dead. As he walks down the drive way he calls for his robot and space ship to find him and pick him up. Eventually the ship turns up, as the police do Benjamin can see the ship even though it is cloaked the hanger bay doors open and Benjamin steps aboard.
BENJAMIN:" Robot you are cutting it fine where have you been."
ROBOT:" Err yes well' I could not find you, bad weather. |"
As Benjamin talks to his computer tell it to record the and wants a picture of the dead target the chief, a close of the body. Once it had been taken out of the house. There are more and more cars coming and the colonel had turned up also. This make Benjamin believe that there on to him again Benjamin must make a session and quick.
Benjamin knows that they know that he can be invisible as for the last time they met.
OXYGEN:" I want you to search the whole area I believe that he is still in the area."
The hitman walks in to the house he could visualized every that had happened he could even see the image of the body before and after it

was deceased. It looked like it was a hit to him. After he come s out if the house he walks to the body for one last look. He tells the forensic team to take the body away.
OXYGEN: "Is he dead."
HITMAN: "Yes, two bullets to his chest, killed him instantly."
OXYGEN: "I guess that there no pay rise for us this year."
Hitman: "knock it off this is not a joke.
The two cops finish at the scene and call it off they get back into the car the cool one drives off. The rest of the police so disperse.

As the last police car disappears down the road its silent again, for some strange reason Benjamin decides to stay around on the ground and zoom in to space. After he had taken a good look at everything he come back and get back on to his ship. As he sits down in the cockpit seat he starts dreaming of being under the sea. As Benjamin falls asleep the robot takes control he gives s Benjamin a surprise as he takes the ship back to earth and in to the ocean. The robot plugs the coordinates and within a minute they are off. The robot is getting good he then turns the computer on it ws voice activated and tells it to play some music, classical of course, for the journey. As Benjamin is sleeping they zoom off into the night and eventually finding the earths coast line as they make their way across the ocean and down underneath it to the cold ocean floor as the robot settles the ship Benjamin wakes up in his favourite place. He was not particular happy but thank full.

He sits up in his seat and watches the life underneath the sea.
As Benjamin is under the sea he sees what is happening to the ocean as he watches what was a left of the wild life. It ws so peace full. Benjamin thanks the robot for taking him there. Benjamin is taking to the Ron=bot and computer about what it would be like to dive and opens a discussion with the booth of them one that he thought would win but he does not. Benjamin is telling the robot that he wants to

explore the ocean the robot does not think much of Benjamin s request. The robot tells Benjamin it could probably take a few years it was a vast place. Benjamin finally gives in and tells the robot the it was a silly thought and he was right they had no time Benjamin is disappointed.

As he slumps back into his chair and continues to watch the sea life around him the robot goes off for a re-charge.

CHAPTER TWELVE
TIME TO PARTY

Benjamin is desperate to know what it would like to swim under the ocean. He is drawn by it beauty and its power Benjamin so despite top know what it would be like to swim under the ocean. He is drawn in by its beauty and its power he could see it and dream about it all day long.
Erich what he was doing. He calls to his computer he is casemated and tells it to find some pitchers Benjamin was busy trying to find what the humans called deep sea diving. Benjamin see=tidy's what we call deep sea divers. Benjamin watches and study the information that the commuter brings to him. Intensively and delighted after wards he goes to his cargo bay looking for some oxygen tanks which he had just seen on serein via his computer, he does not have any. He is disappointed

there ws only one way od's =f doing this and that was going back up to the earths surface and finding land.

Benjamin was excited about what he was he might be doing in the future. he searches for another things way=his robot. Eventually he finds s a surf shop which would sell diving equipment. As he speaks to hides robot.

BENJAMIN: "Is this stuff good."

ROBOT: "Yeah it is safe just do not take the mouth piece out of your mouth. Or you will drown."

BENJAMIN: "Drown."

ROBOT: "Yes drown, you will suffocate."

BENJAMIN:" Explain again

ROBOT: "There is nothing to it once you have your suit on you just put the tank which is full of oxygen that's is h2o on your back over your suit. Then all you will do is jump into the water but remember that you can only breathe through the mouth piece without it you will suffocate and probably drown."

BENJAMIN:" That does not sound very nice."

ROBOT: "If you drown that will be the end of you, so be careful."

Benjamin is still a little confused but thinks he understands the ins and the outs of it. Benjamin leans back in his chair with the look of delight in his face. he was getting e3xcited, the sun flowers had started to laugh, and morality seems the same he was happy too.

Although there were still a few things on Benjamin's mind like the next job and the cops that were following him around knowing that the cops knew that all the murders were all linked and were pray=try close on catching him how ever Benjamin already knew this. Benjamin wants the facts as he -sends his mind back into the past he treys to re-call the insolent on the roof on top of the building and when he was stuck in between them one of them mentioned a name.

Benjamin thinks and thinks until he is confused in his mind and finds the answer that he ws looking for now knowing that the cops were trailing him. Benjamin closes his eyes and within a few minutes find s him that was easy Benjamin says his name to himself. Oxygen. That was what he was called Benjamin has found one of the cops.

Benjamin ws now thinking that he can use the name of the cop to hack into the city. Of course, blaming the cop. As Benjamin also now knows that he is being followed beaming wants to know how close to

them he was and was thinking weather or not he was in the position of being caught.
COMPUTER:" There is an eighty percent chance that you will get caught."
BENJAMIN; "Even if we are under the water."
COMPUTER:" Yes unfortunately."
Benjamin sighs.
BENJAMIN:" Computer give me everything that you have on the oxygen."
The computer bilges the cop has two names and his address with some other personal stuff comes up onto the screen his cars number plate stating that they both drive fast. Benjamin believes that the information came up on to the computer t=way too quickly they wanted to be found or that they were extremely stupid.

Benjamin has a massive profile on his screen in front of him of the copper they call oxygen on the planet earth. Benjamin has everything from his shoes size to the colour of his underpants, to the colour of his eyes. Benjamin is beginning to enjoy himself, but back on the planet the cops are following Benjamin's last hit and thinking about the fourth. As they try and figure out if there is a pattern and who is Benjamin's next victim. It was a priest who ever was trying to tip him off was going a good job. The cool one had a good system to Benjamin's robot there engineering was similar. I should have mentioned it earlier they both did things when they were commanded. This time h=the hint=am nans d the oxygen was taking the murders more seriously especially this one. They were going to guard the victim the priest. As the priest was just leaving the chapel, all they had to do is approach him, as he closed the doors, oxygen was making an approach not knowing that the man was going to run. The priest was quick, and the oxygen was in grabbing distance it was not long before oxygen had run out of oxygen.
Oxygen:" Boy, that guys quick."
Oxygen fails to make the arrest, he knows not to shout at him as there might be people listening.
The oxygen takes a breath and continues as the hitman with him a full-on chase begins as they are now side by side sprinting down the grave yard and down some wonky paths in to disused fields and back on to the main roads they stop knowing that they had lost him. In the end when they could run no more they both shout out. The priest still does not know that he is a target. As the priest runs off obviously not wanting to talk oxygen opens a discussion and starts a debate he continues that there could have been a hundred reasons why he ran. He continues that he was obviously scared of something. as the priest ran not wanting to talk to the police. Not realizing that he was in danger, he runs in to town which was near there was more people there and it was easier for him to hide. Ass he stops to gather his breath looking over his shoulder their ws nobody following him yet. He walks in to a clothe s shop looking for some normal clothes. He decides s to by a jacket it was a girl's jacket and it would work whoever was following him was clearly looking for some one wearing black. He then went for

dome shoe s grabbing any pair that was different to what he was wearing. Not caring if they fitted or not. Oxygen was right behind him, the priest thought that he had out run them but in fact it was the opposite. The col one was a seriously fast verse. The priest looked like he had been court. As he was pushed in to the super verse he was not happy ensure why they were arresting him. after they had begun to drive the oxygen explains they both try to explain to him that he was in danger, the p [rest opposites for running and he goes into shock when find s out that he is a target a hit. The man asks if he can get out of the car as he claimed to feel sick the oxygen pulls over in a busy street the man get out of the car a ND is sick then with in a second he runs off. The hitman could have seen that move coming it was a classical movie stunt. They are both quick enough to act. They both get out of the cool one and phaser him. The priest falls to the floor in pain and passes out completely.

The two cops pick him up and puts him in side the col one. He is cuff for his own protection.

The man is unsettled and wants answers that the oxygen does not have. In the end he just shuts up not saying anything. They knew that he was going to run off gain and the truth is that they needed him and could use him for bate which was what was happening. The priset wanted something to drink and was asking for a beer. The hitman is persuaded and says yes if it calms him down. Toney both tell him to shut up as he had not stopped talking for an hour.

The oxygen finally gets him calm enough to tell him the truth. Oxygen:" just shut up and be quiet we have a lot riding on you."
The priest answers. With holy verb and then continues to the pint of throwing the cup and ripping off the toilet seat and chucking at the cell only rot upset himself more. Everybody ib the office at that point tells him to shut up. The priest passes out at that moment on the cell bed and did not wake up until a few hours later. Only for the fact that he was being slapped awake and did not awake full until a jug of water had been poured upon him. They were back on track least they thought they were. The hitman puts the man back into the car and drive him

home. the oxygen believes that he now safe the oxygen leaves his side and are parked within walking distance of the priest.

Meantime the hitman is being followed by the Benjamin and heist getting real close he is right behind him up to his front door. With the oxygen not around the hitman had left himself in a vulnerable position. Benjamin pulls his weapon the hitman was prised Benjamin tells him not to turn around. The hitman quietly asks Benjamin what he wants. Benjamin tells him that he wants him to stop following him around. The hitman taking all his bottle turns a round knowing that he could be killed, but Benjamin was not there. The hitman is in shock and is trying to locate Benjamin he knows not to move at that point but looks real hard into the darkness. The hitman finally calls the brief encounter in and with an hour the oxygen was by his side. They discuss what had happened. The oxygen was telling the hitman that Benjamin could not kill in cold blood why he did not know in all his victims they all the same they had all killed somebody.
After that conversation the hitman started to argue as the thought of having Benjamin behind him tat close was upsetting him. The argument a=was a long one. The oxygen was on the receiving end of it. The hitman tells oxygen he could have been shot the hitman continues the hitman was quizzed n why Benjamin did not kill him.

The hitman replies that that he was a wanted criminal and heed did not kill him did the oxygen understand. The hitman had no more answers for the moment. Then suggested that his partner the oxygen had been brain washed the oxygen was extremely un happy about what his partner had said they brawl for a minute of=r two the hitman coming in second place as the oxygen would not release him from a head lock until he gave him an apology

Oxygen:" is that it you're going to give in just like that for a treat so what it is part of the job."
The hitman was scared for the first time. Oxygen could finally see it. in the end the two cops part oxygen tell the hitman that he will see him tomorrow and what ever happened this evening was over and done. The hitman closes his door and the oxygen in the cool one slams his shut tight. It was not a good idea to leave the hitman on his own, so the oxygen pulls up down the road and turns the cool one around facing the hitman's house making sue=re that he is safe for the rest of the night.
Benjamin was busy looking for the priest he had already scoped the whole town out thinking that he went some where busy he was on the right tracks the priest was back at his home and Benjamin found him again purely by chance. As he was following his trail he had no idea that he was going to bump straight in to the man meanwhile the hitman still trying to gr=et over the other night and at this time had no concern for the priest.
Benjamin:" hay nice clothes."
The priest:" yeah reasonable."
They look at each other. They both realize that there is something familiar about the situation.
The priest:" do I know you."
Benjamin:" no I do not believe that we have met."
Benjamin knows exactly who he was talking to and shortly after the priest knew too Benjamin did not make the hit straight away, but it was only a matter of time. Just as beaming had disappeared in to the crowed of shoppers the hitman turns up the priest at that point gave the hitman Benjamin's directions. The hitman also goes in to the crowed.

In the end Benjamin stops and turns around he can clearly see the hitman Benjamin shout at him telling him to raise his weapon. The hitman understands him as the people depart making a small lie down the middle of the street people either side of them. Benjamin tells the hitman not to take him for a fool and tells him to go for his gun. The hitman takes another step forward Benjamin is watching the priest is getting excited. As he is speaking to Benjamin steadying his hand. Benjamin knows now that he has been found. He does not take prisoners they both step out in the street. Exciting the people around them even more including the priest. It was a duel. Benjamin has the upper hand as he could morph. The hitman did not waist anytime he fire s first lucky for brinkman that he had only hit his badge. It was enough pressure to force Benjamin off his feet and on to his back. As Benjamin get up he morphed into a tiger. The hitman does not see him coming he was that fast.

Benjamin is happy to continue the hitman does not believe what he is seeing. As he has nonknowledge of the badge Benjamin morphs himself back into himself. The hitman ire's another shot as he pushes the priest over to get him out of the way, so he cannot be harmed fires another shot again not forgetting that he was not the target, but the priest was. As the hitman's shots miss as he falls backwards on to the floor unloading his cartage until it is empty. Giving Benjamin a chance to get on top off him the hitman believes that he going to die and closes his eyes Benjamin sees the priest the real target morphing himself back raises his phaser and shoots the priest dead. The dead body falls to the floor. Benjamin knows that the job was done, the people gather around the cop and the priest in silence and shock. Benjamin is on his way home again.

The priest was dead, and the hitman was alive Benjamin tells his robot it should have been the other way around.
The last three targets that Benjamin was thinking about even before he praised the dead priest had come into mind. They would not be easy. It felt weird to walk on planet earth as within a few hundred yeas it would not be here. It might be destroyed. The earthlings did not have the technology.as I walked from street to street I eventually found my space ship. Benjamin was happy to greet on board. This time I took it up above the planet and hovered there in and above the clouds.

Benjamin fell asleep fast and his robot was in control and the next morning he awoke me. as I was waking up asked the computer for the facts. It put them in front of me on my computer screen. I could clearly see everything that I had done. After I was trying not to think about it to much.
Benjamin is happy to continue.

CHAPTER THIRTEEN
IT TAKE TWO TO TANGO

I was fresh out of ideas I had just met the man who was going to end my life I di not know why I did not kill him myself. I guess it takes two to tango, the priest target was dead I was wondering when it would be my turn. I was feeling very little remorse over the targets position I was glad that he was dead. Benjamin was still getting to terms of the in and the outs of his job. He also knows that he is being used. He was like the robot with no real feeling. He knows that he is being used as a machine. Benjamin flees to the bottom of the ocean knowing that his feminise are still up there.

END OF PART ONE

Add your Book Title

Add your Author Name

Published in 2017 by FeedARead.com Publishing

Copyright © The author as named on the book cover.

First Edition

The author has asserted their moral right under the
Copyright, Designs and Patents Act, 1988, to be identified
as the author of this work.

All Rights reserved. No part of this publication may be reproduced,
copied, stored in a retrieval system, or transmitted, in any form or by
any means, without the prior written consent of the copyright holder,
nor be otherwise circulated in any form of binding or cover other than
that in which it is published and without a similar condition being
imposed on the subsequent purchaser.

A CIP catalogue record for this title is available from the British
Library.

Chapter One